Provence

THE TRADITION OF CRAFT AND DESIGN

Provence

THE TRADITION OF CRAFT AND DESIGN

Amelia Saint George

conran
OCTOPUS

To Alexander, my thanks.

First published in Great Britain in 2000
by Conran Octopus Limited
A part of Octopus Publishing Group
2-4 Heron Quays, London E14 4JP

Text copyright © Amelia Saint George 2000
Design and layout copyright © Conran Octopus
    Limited 2000
Special photography copyright © 2000
    Yves Duronsoy, Michelle Garrett
    and Helen Fickling.

Commissioning Editor Denny Hemming
Managing Editor Catriona Woodburn
Project Editor Helen Huckle
Copy Editor Barbara Mellor
Art Editor Isabel de Cordova
Picture Researcher Rachel Davies
Production Controller Alex Wiltshire

British Library Cataloguing-in-Publication
Data. A catalogue record for this book
is available from the British Library.

ISBN 1-84091-088-7

Colour origination by Sang Choy International,
Singapore. Printed in China.

half-title: A *pétanque* player awaits his turn.
page 2: Fields of sunflowers make a spectacular sight.
The seedheads are harvested to make sunflower oil.
title: Black olives are picked with hand-held rakes when
they are fully ripened, from December to February.
contents, right: A sheet of poppies covers fallow ground.
Poppy seeds are used in baking, or to make artists' oils.
contents, far right: Craftsmen such as Ernest Dettinger
in Vallabrègues still practise the art of enclosing glass
wine casks in protective and portable basketry.

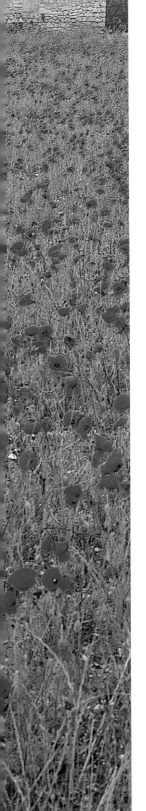

contents

Lying between the Rhône river and the Italian border, Provence was known to the Ancient Greeks, who introduced the vine and the olive through the ports of Massalia – Marseille – and Nice. The Romans established their first settlement in 122BC at Aquae Sextiae – Aix-en-Provence – and called the new province Provincia, seeing it as a useful stepping stone between Italy and Spain. Proclaimed a kingdom in AD879, it later became part of the Holy Roman Empire and eventually, in 1481, part of France. From the Middle Ages onwards, wave upon wave of influences flowed through the Mediterranean ports, from Algeria, Tunisia, Egypt, Turkey and Greece, introducing many diverse arts and crafts that are the source of today's traditions. Down the centuries, artists, drawn to the region by its exceptional light, have worked not only on canvas but on other materials – Picasso on glass and pottery, Matisse on ceramic and stained glass, Chagall on mosaic.

introduction

opposite The impressive ruins of the medieval citadel above Les Baux-de-Provence.
above The vaulted ceiling of the Chapelle Saint Martial in the Palais des Papes, Avignon, painted by Matteo Giovanetti.

top A simple
fil-de-fer basket hangs
on a shutter restraint.

above Woven filter
mats, or *scourtons*,
are used in olive
presses both ancient
and modern.

right Stacks
of hand-thrown
terracotta flowerpots
at Poteries Ravel.

Traditional arts and crafts, some of which have only been revived since World War II, are now practised once more throughout Provence, using local materials and experience. The exceptional ceramic tiles of Alain and Jacotte Vagh in Salernes, the wonderful Provençal Souleiado prints made by the Deméry family in Tarascon, the elegant embroidery of Edith Mézard, and the inviting, rush-seated chairs of Bruno Carles are all examples of contemporary crafts people maintaining the expertise of their forefathers.

Although I have visited Provence continually over the years, now that I live here, I find the region and its people and culture, and the history of both its fine art and its decorative arts, even more fascinating and rewarding than I could have imagined. In this book, I am delighted to have the opportunity not only to show some exceptional interiors created with care, but also to meet crafts people in their homes and workplaces, so introducing the reader to their skills, their environment and their wealth of experience.

Incorporating Provençal style within any home gives scope for playing with colours, from the brightest of primaries to the subtlest of natural tones. Natural materials are a characteristic feature of Provençal interiors, including metal; cane and rush; carved and painted wood; tiled floors in terracotta or vivid glazes; fabrics from embroidered linen to quilted *boutis*, and from Souleiado prints to gauzes. This book explains traditional methods of installation, cleaning and usage, while exploring a range of design ideas.

Provence, the Tradition of Craft and Design, is a book of traditional ideas that work well in contemporary interiors around the world, as they are of good quality in materials that have stood the test of generations. Refurbishing my own Provençal house to its original design has meant that I have been able to experiment with the projects described, whether painting a wooden chair or making chair covers, designing and making a *boutis* cushion, or laying tiles. I have learnt directly from the people who practise these crafts today, working with the finest of natural materials and using techniques that have been honed to perfection. They have been generous enough to share with me not only their experience and expertise, but also their special insights and the tricks of their particular trade – to your best advantage and mine.

above Dipped candles dry between the twenty dips necessary to create long candles, at La Ciergerie des Prémontrés in Graveson.

left Antique Provençal 'trapped bubble' glass in the Souleiado museum in Tarascon.

The geological origins of ochre – sandy clay deposits coloured with iron oxide – can be traced back over one hundred million years. Although many countries have natural deposits, the rarest ochres are those containing every nuance from deepest red to glowing yellow.

The village of Roussillon and its surroundings, midway between Apt and Gordes in the Vaucluse, offer the most staggering views of raw cliff faces striated with colours, ranging from creamy yellow to deep magenta. Here the Sentier des Ocres route runs through a spectacular landscape of walls and peaks of dramatic colour, sculpted as much by erosion as by human excavation. The ochre mines of the Vaucluse are still considered the most important in the Western world, unique for the depth, breadth and variety of their cliff deposits. From these ochres come the pigments used to make paints in rich earth colours, early examples of which have been discovered in cave dwellings in several areas of the Vaucluse. **pigment**

opposite No modern paint could rival the ochre-based colour of this wall as it fades over the years.
above Even the brightest natural-pigment shades will eventually mellow in the Provençal sun.

Ochre has been used for centuries to paint buildings, frescoes and *trompe-l'oeils* murals. Its rich colour proved relatively resistant to light, and could be fixed with binding media such as blood, egg and fat, making it exceptionally versatile. Even today the raw sand is still used to make *crépi*, a coloured wall-rendering that is inexpensive and durable. One of the simplest paints to make is a mixture of pigment, milk and ground lime, known as 'whitewash', a coat of which was traditionally applied each Easter Sunday to freshen up the front of the house. The changing mixtures over the years and natural weathering have combined to produce some charming effects.

Cliffs of blood and gold

The magnificence of the landscape around the village of Roussillon and the warm, rich colouring of its houses are due to the 17 shades of ochre found locally, notably in the breathtaking former quarries

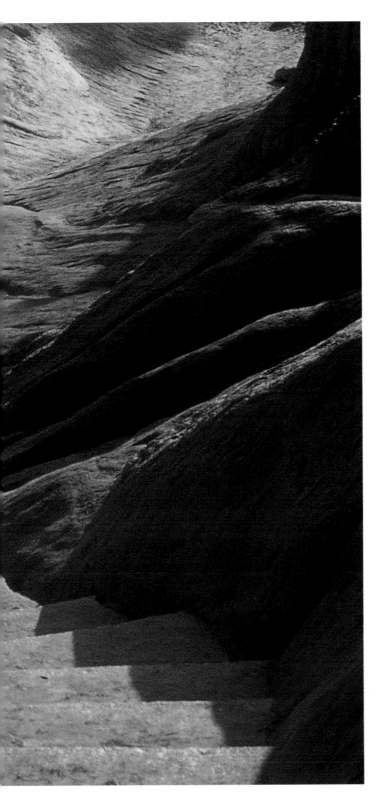

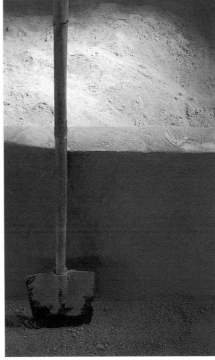

opposite Roussillon, perched on its coloured cliff tops.

centre The earth is stained every shade from yellow to red according to its iron oxide content.

left A spade stands as witness to the former activity in the old Mathieu factory.

of the immense Chaussée des Géants, or Giants' Causeway. The quarries are situated mainly to the south-east of the village and walking routes are sign-posted (rough clothes and old shoes are recommended). A car trip for the non-walkers or a long hike for the enthusiast will reveal the amazing cliffs of the Val des Fées or Valley of the Fairies, to the south. Not for nothing were these cliffs dubbed 'Les Falaises du Sang et d'Or', or Cliffs of Blood and Gold.

A visit to Roussillon in the rain is a treat. The cliffs are even more spectacular and the sandy water gushes over the roads in thick coats of colour – though for safety reasons the quarry walks are closed. Perched high on the cliffs, the village is a charming collection of houses clustered together. Some houses are of natural stone, but most are rendered in the deepest hues – rust reds, burnt sienna, yellow ochre and even crimson. The rule for choosing a house colour in Provence is that it should be of the local earth, and in Roussillon these strong tones work well

together. The stone houses also reveal different colours, both in the stones themselves, which range from burgundy through red, grey and cream to vivid yellow, and in the differing hues of the mortar, to which repairs have been made over the years, resulting in a stunning patchwork of colour.

A declining industry

The history of ochre extraction in Provence began in 1785 when Jean-Etienne Astier, a wood gatherer in the hills of Roussillon, registered himself as an 'ochre manufacturer'. Astier's intuition paid off as he transformed Roussillon's relatively low-grade ore into sought-after pigments for preparing dyes, through a process of grinding, mixing, washing, decanting and drying. The Vaucluse mountains provided him with plenty of water for washing the ochre, which could then be left to dry in the warm air. In the traditional method of manufacture, the ochre was placed in running water to wash out the sands. The precious residue, or *fleur*, was then washed again, cut in pieces, dried and powdered ready for sale. After Astier obtained authorization to grind the pigment in the village oil mill, his business became viable. By 1810 he was running three factories and competing with others seeking to emulate his success. When railways replaced mules for transporting the ochre from the mountain to the coast, business took off, reaching a peak extraction rate of 40,000 tonnes in 1929. But with the introduction of ferrite, a synthetic substitute of American origin, production declined to present-day levels, with only one remaining factory producing ochre and offering educational visits and workshops in summer.

As you travel the countryside, you will see depots of building materials for sale: gravel or split rocks; large grey rounded rocks from the deeper bed of the Durance river; and smaller grey pebbles from the river banks. Besides these will be heaps of sands, some as pale as milk, others the colours of butter, and – the most stunning of all – the deep rich rust sand from Roussillon.

Making coloured render

Apart from the sheer childish delight of mixing your own colours with sand, this is one occasion when you can go wild with colours, as they dry to softer hues – only to reveal their true density again when it rains. To experiment with making render suitable for an outside wall, mix white cement and different-coloured sands with water and apply the resulting mixtures to the wall with a wooden plaster trowel. Make several test samples and leave them for a few days, carefully noting the proportions used, as the colour becomes much lighter as the render dries. My final recipe was a child's bucket of coloured sand to one full-sized bucket of white cement and another of milk-coloured sand.

When you have decided on your mixture, wet the trowel and cover the wall with sweeping windscreen-wiper movements. Home-made renders are excellent for applying directly onto walls made from inexpensive but unattractive breeze blocks, giving a pleasing effect for little outlay. If you do not finish the work in one day, simply make up the same recipe on the following day.

opposite The *crépi* on this arch has peeled to reveal the stone beneath – in harmony with the shades of ochre beyond.

left A newly painted house stands out, but the colours will soften with the passing seasons.

Ranging from oval bull's-eye windows to lofty arches, they are majestic and extremely tempting – but you should be wary of buying expensive 'antique' stone, as it is relatively easy to falsely 'age' most stone.

The architecture of Provence has been determined largely by the surprisingly fierce weather, alternating mistral wind and scorching sun. In towns and villages alike, houses cluster together against the elements, while in the open countryside, thick stone walls, small windows and reinforced doors protect the inhabitants from the biting wind. Isolated farmhouses, or *mas*, were usually built on a rectangular plan, with additions grafted on when needed. Larger houses, or *bastides*, are slightly more formal in style, with more detail and symmetry. Both are traditionally built of stone, with thick wooden shutters and their larger windows facing south. North-facing walls are lower, and the roof is extended over the lower outbuildings, originally stables or storage for grain or farm machinery, and now often converted to garages. The sunnier southern side of the house was often planted with a row of plane trees, to provide valuable shade. It is here that you will find decorated door frames and windows and pretty balconies, often with a sundial on the wall and a tiled dovecote beyond.

The most ancient dwellings in Provence are *bories* – small, low, domed buildings made simply from stacked limestone slabs with no mortar. Found throughout Provence, *bories* are still used for storage and temporary shelter for farmers and shepherds. The village of Gordes has restored an ancient cluster of 20 *bories*, dating from 3500BC. In the low-lying Camargue, home for both herdsmen and salt-gatherers was traditionally a long, low structure with a rounded end facing north and small shuttered windows to east and west, while the south side revealed a charming façade with larger windows and a door. The walls, made of compressed clay and straw, were limewashed dazzling white beneath a sloping roof thatched with marsh reeds.

Painted exteriors

The towns and villages of Provence boast a wealth of decorative details on the exterior of their buildings. Windows and doors are picked out with raised frames, often in a contrasting colour, while string courses in relief mark the level of the different storeys. Raised window frames are made by tacking a temporary wooden frame to the wall and window opening, and applying within it additional layers of rendering until they are flush with the shuttering, which is then removed.

The most elaborate window and door ornaments are in carved stone, and are to be seen mainly in once-important market towns that are now, happily, being restored to their former beauty. When a building is demolished, such ornamental features may be bought by antique dealers or architectural salvage yards.

Sign-writing

Sign-writing is an unmissable tradition in Provençal villages, with weathered and faded lettering standing as a pleasant reminder of former commerces. Even today, with sprawling hypermarkets and their flashing neon lights banished to the outskirts of towns or motorway junctions, the only conspicuous advertising in villages is the traditional green-cross light of the pharmacy.

The sign-painter's craft is both economical and individual. A big advertiser such as Pernod 51 would supply a tracing that was used to place the letters directly onto an outside wall where the idiosyncracies of each building meant that the advertisement appeared differently every time. The letters were filled in with paint and in the autumn sealed with wax, giving an initial sheen to the letters which faded in the sun the following summer. Some enlightened village and town councils are now looking to revive the use of painted wall signs, shunning modern plastic and metal advertising panels that dangle and turn in the breeze. Gaily printed parasols and chairs have now appeared as a substitute, clustered around café tables, and sign-writers are relearning old skills and applying their craft all over walls and new shop fronts. They also design many of the newer sundials, frequently using time-honoured inscriptions such as:

Comptez les heures de soleil.
Count the sunny hours.

Profitez de tout beau moment, car il ne revient pas.
Profit from each good moment, as it cannot return.

Laissez parler les autres de tempêtes et d'averses
Moi, je ne marque que les heures ensoleillées.
Let others tell of storms and showers
I only mark the sunny hours.

opposite The memory of a long-vanished shoe manufacturer lingers on.

left Once at the cutting edge of *la publicité*, an advertisement for Dubonnet now fades in glorious ultramarine.

right A *trompe-l'oeil* draped curtain is a masterful trick. Many people have been deceived into attempting to feel the texture of the fabric.

Trompe-l'oeil

Provence has a rich history of *trompe-l'oeil* paintings, which are to be found in all sorts of settings, from simple homes to palaces. *Trompe-l'oeil* painting gives the illusion of perspective where there is none. Flat walls are transformed into moulded plaster panelling, windows are enhanced with draped curtains that cannot swing in the breeze, and a never-to-be-used coat hangs by the kitchen door. I once even bent down to pick up a banknote on a friend's front doorstep, only to find it did not exist! *Trompe-l'oeil* can offer panoramic views from rooms that deserve expansive aspects but have tiny windows or even no external walls, and it can be the key to turning a drab space into an interior of interest and presence. Equally, it can introduce a little fun into sober surroundings. The basic tenet of successful *trompe-l'oeil*, however, is that the subject should be believable. Many creative *trompe-l'oeil* artists start with an element that is perfectly in context, such as a door frame, before seducing the viewer into a world of the imagination.

A revival of the traditional use of pigments played an important part in the recent restoration of the Palais des Papes, the palace built in Avignon in the fourteenth century for the fugitive popes from Rome. Here, *trompe-l'oeil* paintings from different periods offer an insight into the priorities of contemporary life. *Trompe-l'oeil* banqueting-tables, seductive gardens and views of the hunt transform the palace walls. Each room has a different theme. In the Pope's bedroom *trompe-l'oeil* stucco columns, now softened with age, are adorned with hanging birdcages in a charming addition to the architectural detail. In the Chapelle Saint-Martial, frescoes painted in 1344 and 1345 by Matteo Giovanetti play with *trompe-l'oeil* perspective for the depiction of buildings among the high vaulted ceilings, but abandon it altogether for the numerous figures. The effect is chaotic but intriguing, a dazzling scene set against a ceiling of deepest ultramarine, scattered with stars in gold leaf.

left Painted sundials are a feature of many houses in Haute Provence, where the tradition of painted furniture is equally strong.

below The simple perspective of faded balustrades and arcades suggests a spaciousness that is both ethereal and illusory.

right Yellow ochre combines well with the local stone and ceramics.

far right Deep pink and yellow make a fiery contrast.

opposite A typical Provençal staircase, with *tomettes* retained by oak batons. Tones of rust and tomato make a warm, rich setting for the stone steps beneath.

Earth colours

Shades ranging from warm rust through to yellow ochre are the hallmarks of Provence. The luminous quality of the Provençal light and the brilliance of its colours have inspired many of the most original painters of the nineteenth and twentieth centuries. Cézanne, a native of Aix, and Van Gogh, a convert to Arles, were both fired by the vibrant shades of the landscape. Early arrivals to the region among the Impressionist painters were Monet and Renoir, to be followed in turn by Bonnard, Signac and Dufy. Picasso chose to spend a great deal of his time in Provence, finally settling near Aix on the slopes of Montagne Sainte Victoire. A museum in Antibes is dedicated to his work. Matisse also captured the Provençal light through his daring use of colours: his work can still be seen today in the seventeenth-century Villa Arson in Nice (note, too, the *trompe-l'oeil* decorative stonework of the villa's façade).

Despite all the hours of sunshine, and the summer visitor's view of Provence as dry and sunny, many houses are very damp. Excess water is a problem, and many houses have wells within the walls to obtain water in summer and to drain it away in winter – or at least to pump it down to a level to avoid flooding. The soil of Provence has a clay base, and the idea of this system is to keep the foundations moist, and avoid drought or flood. With rising damp thus a continual presence in older homes, it has been the fashion for centuries to paint the walls with layer upon layer of inexpensive limewash. While acrylic and oil paints are durable in most conditions, on damp walls they simply buckle and peel off.

As it is not always feasible to grind your own pigment for this finish, a company called Blancolor has created a new subtle range of colours that can be mixed to create that perfect shade, so encouraging a return to the use of traditional paints and pigments.

Painted interiors

Softer tones are sometimes called for indoors. Passages and
stairways that might be phenomenal in deepest ochre can be soft
and relaxing in more mellow tones – unless, like Blancolor's owner,
you have five small children, when, as he ruefully admits, pale
walls are a dream best saved for old age.

Pale hues are easily combined to produce very subtle effects.
Chaste white can be a problem if you have young children or
animals, or visitors who insist on squashing mosquitoes over the
walls, but there is no denying that pure white walls, unbleached
linen, natural beige cushions, pale rush seating and soft white

painted furniture together create an atmosphere of serene – if somewhat impractical – elegance.

A clever Provençal idea is the placing of one or more strips of masking tape horizontally and vertically around the room before painting, creating an effect similar to a dado, but including doors and windows. Complementary or contrasting shades are then painted above and below the tape, and the resulting bands or blocks of colour add depth and interest to the walls. The method for incorporating windows is similar to that for creating an external frame (see page 16), but this time within the room, so lending increased space and importance to the window area.

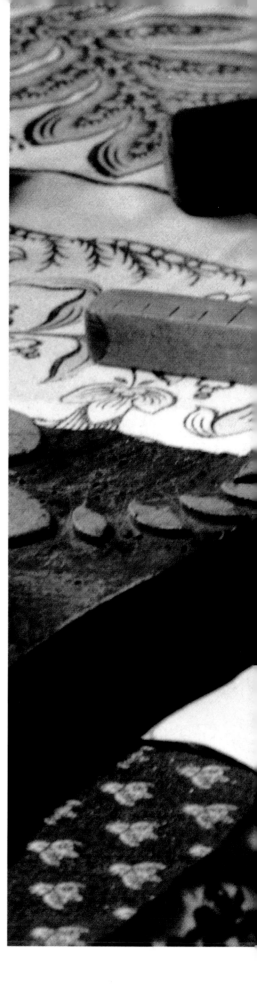

fabric printing

Printing on fabric is a centuries-old technique of combining inks with a pattern. In Provence, intricate designs based on native fruit and flowers were traditionally cut from fruit-wood blocks. For fine line detail, copper sheeting was inserted into the block, and nail heads of varying dimensions were used to make points or dots. Dyes were obtained from a variety of sources: highly valued indigo, a dark blue with violet hues, was imported from India or extracted from the leaves of the *ingotier* or wood bush, and other vegetable dyes were extracted from local plants and berries. While a few colours were fast when washed, many of the vegetable dyes washed away, leaving only a shadow of their original colour, much as red wine leaves a dull brown stain. It was not until the East India Company sent a spy to India in 1734 that it was discovered that the dyes were good, but the technique of printing required mordants, or metallic salts, to 'bite' into the fabric. The combination of metallic salts and vegetable dyes was then mixed with gum arabic. This allowed the dyes to penetrate the fabric fibres, impregnating them with stain, while the gum arabic thickened the solution, avoiding the running and bleeding that gave a smudged effect to the block print. In this way a washable fabric could retain an exceptional print impression. The original blocks can still be seen in the Souleiado factory, where they are used in a variety of combinations to create new designs.

above right Traditional pigments are derived from natural sources, including many plants. Curcuma, or turmeric, yields a brilliant saffron yellow.

centre The depth and richness of the Souleiado fabrics are the result of a process in which five separate printing blocks are used to build up the intricate designs.

below top Copper
measuring pans hang
over the sink in the
Souleiado pigment-
mixing kitchen.

below bottom
Measuring utensils with
spattered test colours
dripping down the
windowpane behind.

trompe-l'oeil hall

This *trompe-l'oeil* panelling was inspired by other elements within the room: the basic shape was taken from the walnut doors, typical of the Aix region, while the detail is copied from the reclaimed banister rail on the hall stairs.

As it is often difficult for the untrained eye to estimate the scale of a finished work, use several pieces of tracing paper for different parts of the design. Move them around on the wall in order to assess the optimum size and position of the design before transferring it. When it comes to painting, I find it useful to use a clockface as a reference for the source of light. The windows in this project are at 10am. Therefore as the light falls on the design, the 10am position will be the lightest and the darker side, or shadow, will be between 2pm and 7pm. Adding shading to achieve an illusion of depth will take the form of a painted straight line for the straight moulding, a crescent moon for the sphere and an oval crescent for the oval form. For the straight, vertical 'mould' design, the shadow falls on each line of the design, with white on the left (10am) side, shading to a mix of raw umber and white on the right (4pm) side. To give the moulding a stronger three-dimensional element, add a raised block crescent in the same 2pm to 7pm position for each sphere to 'sit' on. Rather than using a softened blending for this, use a pre-mixed uniformly darker tone.

materials and tools
pencil,
tracing paper,
masking tape,
good quality acrylic
or oil paints,
good quality
paintbrushes (square,
round and pointed),
tape measure,
spirit level.

step one Sketch your design on paper. Enlarge it to the required size and copy it onto tracing paper. Using a spirit level, establish the position of the design on the wall, then attach the paper design to the wall with masking tape and trace over the lines.

step two Using good quality acrylic or oil paints, mix up a dilute solution of paint. Apply a dilute mix of raw umber and white to the design as a base coat, but do not obliterate the pencil markings. Paint between the lines of the panel with a pointed brush.

step three Paint in all the details in white, with a shadow inference of burnt umber, leaving a highlight each time. Add some further additional shading to the panel base, gradually building up the different forms, and giving each one its individual shadow.

sundial (*cadran solaire*)

materials and tools
newspaper,
paper and pens,
good quality synthetic
plaster (better weather-
resistance and pre-mixed),
spirit level
tracing paper
or carbon paper,
good quality acrylic
or oil paints,
varnish,
compass and protractor,
metal hand of sundial,
masking tape,
paint brush,
sticky putty,
ladder (if necessary)
drill.

Painted sundials brave the elements without the aid of the sculptor's chisel or the blacksmith's furnace: just a paintbrush and a few sketches suffice.

Whatever decorative border you choose for your sundial, the basic pattern will be the same. Position the face using a compass and protractor. Remember that it will be viewed from a distance, and plot the size and shape of your design by placing newspaper on the wall. Sketch the design on paper, beginning with a vertical centre line, then place a cross for the base of the sundial hand: all measurements are taken from this mark. Place the protractor on the cross with 90 degrees pointing down over the centre line. Mark out the degree placements: 20 = 5pm, 38 = 4pm, 52 = 3pm, 66 = 2pm, 78 = 1pm, 90 = 12, 102 = 11am, 114 = 10am, 128 = 9am, 144 = 8am, 160 = 7am.

When working, come down the ladder from time to time to assess your work from below. Use artist's quality oil or very good acrylic paints as the sundial will have to endure all weather conditions. Varnish can add a little protection, but the only effective weatherproofing is resin, which is unpleasant and difficult to apply. When you have finished painting, drill a hole at the marked cross and wedge in the metal hand with sticky putty. Leave for a day or two to check the angle of the needle on hours, ajust if necessary and set firm with plaster.

step one Trace the outer edge of your design onto the wall using a spirit level and apply a rendering of synthetic plaster to level out the wall surface within the design. Let it dry overnight.

step two Trace your design on tracing paper or, better still, place carbon paper behind your paper design and transfer the lines onto the wall, using masking tape to hold the papers in place.

step three Paint in the design, using several layers so that it is absorbed into the plaster and becomes more durable. The colours will also be less uniform, giving a hand-painted finish.

Provence has rich deposits of clay running from Marseille on the coast, inland through the Aixoise region and Aubagne, up to Manosque and into the hills of Salernes. Each region's clay has its own colour and texture. In Aix, the firm of Santon Fouque keeps the clay in a cellar for a year to gather mould, making it more pliable for fashioning tiny *santon* figures. In the Aubagne, the craftsmen of Poteries Ravel mix the clay for their large moulded garden pots so as to obtain a particular soft terracotta hue. Deep-red clay deposits are made into the hexagonal *tomette* tiles that Alain Vagh produces in Salernes, now an instantly recognizable feature of many Provençal interiors. In the hill village of Fayence, the differing colours of local clays are combined to make distinctive marbled ceramics. In the mountains, set on the edge of a ravine, the secluded village of Moustiers is famous for detailed, brightly coloured designs of flora and fauna painted over glazed clay.

ceramics

opposite Distinctive hexagonal *tomette* tiles are practical throughout the house.
above Alain Vagh's tile hunting scene is painted in the soft blues of Moustiers.

Roof tiles

The traditional clay roof tiles of Provence were influenced by Roman design and are still called *tuiles romaines*. Thick red terracotta *tuiles canales* are made in a curved shape so that they can be used either way up, their overlapping joins rendering them weatherproof. Roman tiles are attached to the roof with mortar to withstand the mistral wind.

To ascertain whether a property in Provence has been well and generously constructed, you only have to look at how the building's original roof tiles were laid. If the tiles are laid to their full length with only the slightest of overlaps, the owner was probably running short of money and had begun to economize. Closely stacked roof tiles, with half a tile overlapping another,

indicate that the original house owner was not only generous, but also required a roof that was both weatherproof and provided efficient insulation against the winter cold as well as the intense summer heat.

Another clue to good building can be seen in the eaves of older Provençal houses. Instead of conventional guttering, two, three or even four layers of tiles are set in mortar beneath the final roof tiles, creating substantial eaves known as a *génoise*. The larger the *génoise*, the wealthier the property. When today's inhabitants want to add guttering, however, the protruding *génoise* makes it a very cumbersome procedure. It is now possible to buy ready-made *génoise* in any length for installation on modern houses. Clearly this Provençal tradition is not about to be lost.

opposite left A round tower is skilfully roofed with glazed tiles in autumnal tones.

opposite right The *génoise* on this typical country *bastide* near Aix has two layers.

left Tiles cover not only the roof of a village house but also the chimney stacks, as protection against the ferocious winds and torrential rain of the Provençal winter.

Glazed roof tiles are rarely used in Provence, as the moisture in the tile expands when frozen and cracks the glaze. The choice of colours is so delightful, however, that glazed roof tiles are used near the frost-free coast from Toulon to Nice, where plumbago and palms survive the mild winters. These tiles are still produced at Alain Vagh's factory, and the choice of colours is as broad as for indoor tiles. Glazed roof tiles are generally used on small, low buildings, so the decorative roof can be seen from the main house. They are particularly effective when used on the little round dovecotes with steeply pitched roofs that dot the area. The first glazed-tile roof I ever saw was on the edge of a forest, and I thought at first that the roof was covered with autumn leaves. Using such vibrant colours on a roof can seem overdramatic, but in practice they can have great charm. Beneath the gardens of the Villa Ephrussi de Rothschild in Saint-Jean-Cap-Ferrat, for instance, a glazed-tile roof in green makes an original landmark when viewed from the road and the sea while at the same time blending attractively with the cypress trees below the rose-coloured villa.

Tiles from Salernes

Earth, water, air and fire are the four vital ingredients for tile production. Salernes has vast deposits of rich red clay, the running water essential for production is supplied by the streams that descend from the Hautes Alpes, warm air circulates freely round the stacked tiles to dry them out before firing, and local forests supply abundant fuel to stoke the kilns. Ceramics have been made here since the Bronze Age (1800 to 450BC), making full use of this tremendous natural resource, for the clay lay here in pure abundance, stratified and relatively easily accessible. Until the nineteenth century, tiles were produced solely for local use, but with the rapid development of the main railway lines into Provence, production expanded to reach a wider market, rising to its peak in the early 1900s. With World War I, a whole generation of workers was wiped out, and before the industry could fully recover, World War II and the concurrent decline in traditional building materials dealt it another double blow. In the late 1960s, however, a younger generation of tile manufacturers revived

the ailing industry, introducing new ideas while continuing the age-old traditions. Salernes clay remains one of the purest available, with no added sand or other impurities, and is particularly durable.

In Salernes, Alain Vagh buys in the different coloured clays, keeping them entirely separate. As the batches of clay tiles are removed from the kiln to cool, this diversity becomes apparent, from the palest sandy tones from nearby Apt to the richest red from Salernes's own clay quarries. The typical tile from Salernes is a hexagon, traditionally measuring 10cm (4in) across, called a *tomette*. It is found on nearly every floor, from convent to château, butcher's to *bastide*. But other shapes, such as rectangles, squares or lozenges, are also available in many different sizes. When all tiles were made entirely by hand, the size was kept small as any distortions on larger tiles were difficult to rectify. Nowadays tile factories have some machines, but amazingly traditional hand-made tiles are still produced, helped along by the odd rickety conveyer belt. The clay is rolled out to the required thickness and the shape stamped out with a tool not dissimilar to a large pastry cutter. Each rough edge is softened by a stroke of the fingertip, and the tile is placed on a conveyer belt to dry over heaters until firing. Traditionally, they were laid on wooden boards to dry in the sun over ten to fifteen days.

Following a legal ruling in July 1895, only Salernes tiles can be marked with the Salernes name. The origin of the tiles is still relevant, as inexpensive copies made in Spain are also on sale in Salernes, and the unsuspecting buyer may find, too late, that the tiles crack during winter frosts. The pure clay tiles of Salernes, fired to high temperatures of 980° Celsius and left in the kiln over a day, are resistant to temperature changes.

Alain Vagh came into tile manufacture and design through his wife Jacotte, and the family business has expanded in colourful fashion. Not only do they excel in the production of shaped terracotta tiles, but they also offer the most exceptional choice of

opposite Provençal tiles are made in various shapes and finishes. When laid, the honeycomb effect of *tomettes* – hexagonal tiles from Salernes – makes fine floors for halls, kitchens and bathrooms.

left Each tile is punched out usinga metal cutter, and the raw edges are smoothed out by hand.

beautiful colours. Alain Vagh insists that, while he is responsible for producing the tiles, half their beauty lies in the design flair and skill of the tiler. In her designs, Jacotte is keen to encourage combinations of colours and the juxtaposition of coloured tiles with plain terracotta. While respectful of tradition, she creates floors in a wide range of fresh colours and decorative motifs.

Glazed and decorated tiles

Introducing glazed colour to clay tiles requires two firings, firstly at the terracotta stage and then after the final colour is sprayed on. Because Salernes clay is so red, any finishing colour apart from red, brown and black requires a base coat of white paint before spraying and refiring.

With decorated tiles, the motif is applied in different ways depending on the pattern. One of the oldest techniques for transferring a design is the pinprick method, involving pricking through a tracing-paper design and allowing traces of pigment to colour the surface of the tile. Stencils can be used to build up a more intricate design. Many of the designs at Alain Vagh are completely freehand in technique and have a wonderful flowing

right Flowing movement can be introduced by using tapered tiles, in circles, waves and scallops.

centre Square terracotta tiles are interspersed with small coloured squares to give a traditional yet contemporary feel.

movement. It is not as easy as it appears to paint onto the prepared surface of white glaze, as the glaze acts like blotting paper, absorbing all the paint on the brush. Alain Vagh's skilled craftsworkers undergo a two-year apprenticeship to perfect the technique, in which they steady the wrist on a supporting bar and turn the tile on a rotating base while applying light and continuous brush strokes like skilled Chinese calligraphers.

Moustiers faïence

Inspiration for hand-painted designs, both contemporary and traditional, owes much to the rich heritage of Moustiers, in the heart of the Alpes Maritimes region. In the seventeenth century an Italian monk imparted his knowledge of fine Florentine glazeware to the two Clérissy brothers, one of whom remained in Moustiers while the other set up a factory in Saint-Jean-du-Désert, near Marseille, in 1697. Successive generations of the Clérissy family refined the art of hand-painting fine earthenware, taking their influences from changing fashions, whether copying Chinese Ming Dynasty imports or reproducing a still life of fish direct from the harbour at Marseille.

In 1711, Joseph Calouriste, working at one of the factories in Marseille, developed two distinctive *marques*: one earthenware decorated with wildflowers that looked as if they had been thrown onto the plate, known as *fleurs jetées*; and the highly distinctive mustard-yellow faïence that is now so closely associated with Provence. Proximity to the port of Marseille resulted in interesting commissions, and many entire sets went overseas, fortunately since during the Revolution much of this elegant faïence was destroyed. Moustiers itself, however, tucked in among the mountains, remained a thriving community and is still producing its glazed earthenware today.

left Tiled stairs are edged with oak batons with plaster risers. In affluent houses the first two steps are made of stone and the rest are tiled.

right A traditional combination of yellow ochre and terracotta. Used outside, glazed tiles will blister and crack in winter frosts. Eventually the glaze will start to peel away.

left The same ochre and rust-red colour scheme used inside a kitchen. The placing of tiles on the diagonal is also typically Provençal.

Glazed coloured tiles became more readily available during the 1960s, when many people wanted colourful and easy-to-clean surfaces. Glazed ceramic tiles have fulfilled this requirement ever since. Fashions in colours vary: some years ago lavender was popular, then yellow, and more recently there has been a trend for a combination of white and terracotta. When laid well, glazed-tile work surfaces are a joy to use because they are durable and resistant to heat and minor scratches. They also provide a cool surface on which to prepare meat or pastry.

Making a mosaic

Denis Aune, one of Alain Vagh's tilers, proved to be both charming and inspirational as he explained with great care the numerous ways of combining different colours and shapes of tiles.

Always lay the tiles out first on a flat surface, he urged, look at them and keep rearranging them until you achieve the desired effect: they are not yet stuck down, so do treat this stage in the planning as a game. Denis encourages you to be bold, constantly introducing ever more colours from the exceptional range made by Alain Vagh, and combining the beautiful colours with wonderful swirls and movement in the positioning of the tiles. Some tiles immediately lend themselves to being used on the diagonal – a traditional Provençal favourite – while other tiles look more effective when laid square on.

Though many of these designs and colour combinations would look stunning in gardens and on balconies, Jacotte Vagh is always wary of recommending them for outside use, because winter frosts will inevitably cause the glaze to crack.

The secret of marbling

The marbled clay of Apt, called *terre mêlée* or mixed clay, and *marbre* from Uzès are made by mixing different coloured clays together. Even a small region here may yield up to six different clay colours, from light grey, pale blue and black to deep terracotta, with many subtle hues in between. Each potter keeps his mixture and his sources a closely held secret. Too much mixing produces a uniform grey, so machines are never used. One method is to layer the clays one on top of the other and twist, then stretch the layers, fold and twist again. The more times this process is repeated, the more intricate the marbled effect will be on the finished article (though only a broken fragment will reveal the full intricacy of the work involved to an untrained eye). The prepared clay is rolled out, placed over a mould and left to dry. The shrunken biscuit clay is then glazed and fired.

Whole dinner services used to be made by this technique, with the handles made in contrasting single colours, and perhaps fashioned in the form of branches, with flowers and leaves forming the knobs on the lids. Because of the amount of intense labour involved and the resulting high price of the finished items, few of these elaborate services are now made.

Anduze vases

Anduze, a town to the west of Nîmes, is not in Provence, but its beautiful vases have been adopted by Provençal gardeners for more than twelve generations. The vases vary in size from the very small to those of chest height, produced mainly for the Provençal orangeries. It was in 1610 that a local potter, inspired by Italian Medici pots at a local fair, produced the first vases here. Experimenting by using the local tile kilns, he reproduced the Florentine decorative fruit and flower swags, introducing a distinctive pedestal foot and glazes that reflected the countryside, from deep straw yellow to herb green. Under the Boisset family, production continued unchanged until it stopped in the 1930s. Happily a new signature scratched into the side of the damp vases – *les enfants de Boisset* – announces the continuation of a long

opposite left
A cream glazeware
soup tureen with
Provençal inscription.

opposite centre
A *dourgue à goulot*
was often kept near the
fountain used for drinking
water, or carried full of
wine into the fields to
quench the workers'
thirst. The practical
design allows the jar to
be filled easily and the
contents hygienically
shared, as it can be held
near but not touching
the lips when drinking.

opposite right In the
elaborate technique of
marbled clay, clays of
different colours are
mixed to produce a wide
range of rippled effects.

left *Jardinières* from
Anduze in the Gard
have been used in
Provence for generations
and surviving older
ones are highly prized.
This *jardinière* is both
signed and dated on
one of the few places
where the glaze has
not blistered.

Santons

The French Revolution may have caused the destruction of fine earthenware, but it also led directly to the creation of an enduring Provençal craft, that of the little *santon*. By 1791 large posters prohibiting the celebration of Midnight Mass had appeared in even the most remote of Provençal villages. As religion became dangerous, so the Christmas *crèche* or nativity scene came into people's homes, made from whatever material was on hand (dough for the baker, wood for the carpenter), and little by little *santons* were born. Having made the Holy Family, a donkey, cow, sheep and shepherds and the three wise men, the craftsmen then went on to make members of their own family, neighbours and people working in the village.

Santons are dressed in traditional prints made up into costumes of the Revolutionary period. One of the first plaster moulds was created in 1764 by Lagnel, and by 1934 Santon Fouque could boast nearly 5,000 moulds in varying sizes. Among the most famous is the *Coup de Mistral* figure of an old man with patched trousers and a flowing cape battling against the wind, created by Paul Fouque in 1952. This master craftsman has now retired, and his daughter Mireille continues his work.

The word *santon* is taken from the Provençal *santoun*, meaning 'little saint', and the figurines are treated with great reverence. Local people traditionally collect *santons* group by group, watching the *crèche* grow over the years and generations. The first *foire aux santons* was held on 1 December 1803 at the Cours de Marseille, and since then every Provençal village holds a *santon* fair before Christmas, in addition to its bustling market. In every home the *crèche* is set up and added to from 4 December, to be put back into store on 2 February. Tradition requires that the *crèche* and surroundings be made entirely of natural materials (glitter or plastic are taboo), and with sprigs of olive, scented rosemary and thyme serving as miniature trees, moss as grass and twigs, and lavender and stones for decoration. Prizes are awarded annually according to strict traditional rules: in 1976 Mireille Fouque was awarded the *médaille vermillon* for one of her creations, and in 1968 her father Paul won the 'Best Craftsman of France' gold medal for the best *crèche* in painted terracotta.

opposite far left
The *santon* museum
sign shows the 'Coup de
Mistral' *santon* created
by Paul Fouque.

opposite right Now
retired, Paul Fouque
cannot resist helping out.
His gold medal-winning
crèche is on display at
the workshop in Aix.

above Some larger
santons are made
with a soft body and
fabric costumes.

left A terracotta
shepherd awaits the
painstaking application
of oil paint.

right Abdelkrim, with his distinctive initials AA, specializes in Poteries Ravel's curvaceous forms.

aubagne pottery

One of the tall kiln chimneys that guide you into Aubagne belongs to Poteries Ravel, manufacturers since 1837 of pots ranging from the traditional to the resolutely contemporary. Here soft-hued terracotta pots are planted with citrus trees in the garden, hold the cascading plumbago on the balcony, and are full of sweet-scented jasmine by the door. For large straight-sided models moulds are used: two for an averagely detailed pot, three for more elaborate designs. The clay is thrust into the mould, and a machine like a huge food-mixer then pushes it into every intricate crevice of the mould. Man and machine together strain the mould to the utmost, removing excess clay to lend excellent detail to the traditional relief of swags of fruit, embossed rosettes and linear bands, or to the contemporary, more tactile designs of the well-known designer Gagnère. The pot is then left to dry, separating from the mould by natural shrinkage of 8 per cent. When the mould is removed, the pot is placed on a huge potter's wheel to be trimmed to shape, the neck refined and details

centre The typical Provençal pots are stored to dry slowly.

left Artur carrys a large, moulded terracotta pot, another speciality of Poteries Ravel in Aubagne.

added, before being stamped with the craftsman's initials. Each potter has his speciality and particular touch, and his initials appear on his work next to those of the founder, Ravel. All the pots are left in large rooms to dry slowly and shrink naturally; some are then glazed blue, green or honey yellow. The unglazed pots are all frost resistant, but must be carefully placed outside so they are not turned over by the mistral wind.

The traditional *jarre provençal*, with its generous body and a nipped-in neck to minimize water loss by evaporation, is made on the potter's wheel, as are all the jugs, bowls with fluted edges and large honey pots. Each jar has a ready-measured share of clay and an experienced potter can pull a pot within ten minutes. Abdelkrim learned as a young boy at his father's elbow; now, he maintains, 'they leave school too late, a good potter should start early'. The factory has barely changed in five generations. Today's owners – cousins Pascal and Marion Ravel – are constantly on hand, opening the modern kiln, loading a client's car or supervising large consignments for distribution worldwide.

tiled floor rug

Designs using the varied tones of natural clay can be both subtle and effective when laid as a tiled floor. In this project, several tile rugs break up the floor of a long thin bedroom, correcting the room's proportions and adding interesting detail. When planning your design it is useful to work with the tiles, adjusting the overall design to fit the tiles rather than creating a design on paper that may involve endless cutting to fit the tiles to the pattern. Begin with the border frieze, which can be adjusted later to the layout of the inner section. Here the central design is made up of diagonally laid tiles, and the frieze of contrasting pale and red tiles cut into triangles, with a border of thinner rectangular tiles. Mark tiles that need cutting with a pencil scribble on the part to be discarded. Use a tile-cutting machine with a rotating saw blade cooled with water.

Lay the tiles using a manufacturer's pre-mixed adhesive cement. Check that each tile is in the correct position, and work on a small area at a time. After grouting, wash the completed floor with water and remove any grouting residue with a 50:50 solution of water and nitric acid. Leave the tiles to breathe for at least a month before applying a lustrous finish of equal parts turpentine and linseed oil which will take three to four days to be absorbed. Repeat the procedure and this time leave even longer, or anything placed on the floor will leave a mark.

materials and tools
chalk,
adhesive cement
(pre-mixed),
terracotta tiles,
grouting,
fine sand,
50:50 solution of water
and nitric acid,
50:50 solution of linseed
oil and turpentine,
tape measure,
tile cutter,
plastic notched spatula
(tile adhesive spreader),
set-square,
rubber hammer,
rubber grouting spreader,
cloth, brush.

step one Work out your design using the tiles, moving them around and experimenting. Mark the position of the frieze, using a tape measure and chalk directly on the cement floor. Use a large set-square to create accurate right-angled corners.

step two Working on a small area at a time, spread adhesive on the floor and push each tile into position. Tap in place with a rubber hammer. Align subsequent tiles using a set-square. Lay 2 sides of the frieze before inserting interior tiles. Leave overnight to dry and do not walk on it.

step three Next day, wet the tiles thoroughly. With a rubber grouting spreader, push grouting around to seep into all the joints. Wipe the tiles clean of cement grouting and throw fine sand over it, brushing it into the joints. Let the floor dry for 24 hours, and again – no walking.

mosaic table

materials and tools
circular MDF board,
nail,
pencil on a string,
tape measure,
tile adhesive suitable
for contact with food,
glazed tiles including
1 round and small
mosaic squares for
edging,
water-resistant grouting,
solvent,
colour-tinted varnish,
tile cutter and pincers,
spatula for grouting.

Glazed tiles are available in an exciting range of colours from pale honey to bright maize yellow, from deep rose to tender baby pink, from the striking blues of the depths of the Mediterranean to the clear blue-green of waves that lap the shore, and from deep forest pine to translucent green, not forgetting blacks, whites, amber, mustard and many more. Salernes clay is so red that introducing any glazed colour apart from red, brown or black requires two firings. After the first firing, the terracotta tile is given a white coat before being sprayed with the finishing colour and refired. Designing with coloured tiles offers tremendous scope. Typical Provençal combinations are various shades of ochre with deep bottle greens or soft white, while natural terracotta and white glazed tiles together give a crisp and effective contemporary feel.

Tiles laid in a circle are stunning, lending sweeping movement to a floor or making a cool and solid table-top as suggested here. The same idea can be used to make an impressive cheeseboard or casserole stand. Whatever you choose to make, you will need a supportive wooden base about 2cm (1in) thick for a 60cm (24in) design. The result is both attractive and practical, as the tiles do not need sealing and are easy to wipe and keep clean. Do not leave these designs outside in frosty weather, however, as the tiles will lift off the board.

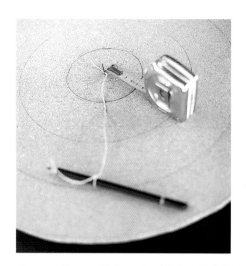

step one Place a nail in the centre of the board to hold the end of a tape measure and a pencil on a string. Trace round the central tile, then mark guiding rings for positioning the rest, using the tape measure to set the distances and allowing 3mm (⅛in) between tiles.

step two Place tiles in the circles, swapping sizes and colours or adjusting spaces until they fit. One by one glue the first ring of tiles into place; most modern glues dry quickly so be sure to place them accurately between your pencil markings. Continue with the second and third rings.

step three With a spatula, apply water-resistant grouting between the tiles for hygienic cleaning; wipe away any smears with a little solvent. Finish the edge of the table-top with small mosaic tiles as here, or seal the wooden board edge with stain or colour-tinted varnish.

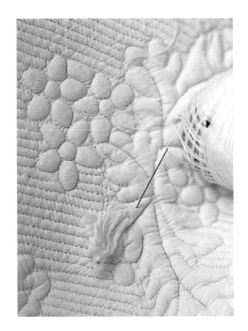

Provençal prints in heavenly colours can be found in every marketplace in the region, with vibrant patterns based on olives and sunflowers, vines and cherries or paisleys and geometrics. '*Les indiennes*', as these gaily printed cottons became known, were first imported from India in the seventeenth century, and have never gone out of favour. Their astonishing early popularity escalated into a mania when they were banned by royal decree, but they also offer solid practical advantages: since the patterns are generally small, there is no repeat and therefore less wastage; and they do not show the dirt, so they are wonderful for children's clothes or tablecloths. The other fabric tradition of Provence offers a more reticent beauty. The incomparable *boutis* – decorative needlework in relief on pure white cotton – is used for cushions and bedspreads for the most elegant of interiors. Older samples, often with coded messages in their designs, are avidly sought by today's collectors. **fabric**

opposite An old quilt, one side a free-flowing design, the reverse a close repeat design in complementary tones.
above A section of chaste white *boutis,* well worn and in need of repair, but still elegant and distinguished.

When *indiennes*, beautiful new cottons in wonderful and, most importantly, fast colours, were imported into Marseille by the East India Company, they rapidly became all the rage at the court of Louis XIV at Versailles. Soon beds, walls, curtains and courtiers alike were covered with the brilliant fabrics. Growing demand gave impetus to a new industry, drawing many silk and wool weavers from Lyon. When the city's textile companies exerted pressure on Louis XIV to ban not only the import of *indiennes* but also production, clandestine factories continued to produce the forbidden fabric, all the more popular for being illicit. But the French were unable to produce colour-fast dyes, and it was not until an East India Company officer engaged in a little industrial espionage that the tricks of the trade were revealed. With the addition of mordants in the form of metallic salts the dyes became colour-fast, and in time the ban was lifted.

Souleiado prints

Although the use of engraved copper rolls was introduced in the early 1900s, the traditional process of hand-block printing lives on at the Souleiado factory museum. Each set of printing blocks consists of one for the outline of the design, followed by a sequence of blocks for the different colours. These are laid on top of the area printed by the first outline block until the design is filled in with all its colours. Very fine lines are produced using an arrangement of cast-metal type or copper strips, as intricate detail would collapse on itself if carved in wood. The background colours, meanwhile, are filled in using plain felt blocks that pick up large amounts of dye and distribute them evenly. A dozen pins, drawn from wire and hammered into the face of a block, will produce pinpoints of colour, and thousands of pins clustered together on one block will print whole forests of shading. Blocks often use different techniques in combination so that one colour may appear printed in a variety of ways, including woodcarving, pins with copper inlays, or felt with metal type.

opposite above A treasured book of sample prints and colourways demonstrating just some of the possibilities within Souleiado's extensive range of designs. Above it are bottles of dyes derived from 'firbuds' and 'orange leaves'.

opposite below An intricate block carved with chisel and gouge. The detailed design is burnt out of the slow-burning lime wood with a red-hot probe fired by a gas burner.

left A kaleidoscope of silk ties in diverse colours and prints, from classical to contemporary, clearly demonstrate the exceptional detail and beauty of the Souleiado designs.

As fashions in fabrics come and go, so the Provençal prints have changed and re-emerged. The vogue from the time of Louis XVI up to the French Revolution was for patterns based on small flowers, herbs and leaves, and these were to flourish again in the flower power decade of the 1970s. The stylized geometric squares and stripes that were fashionable during the Napoleonic period, meanwhile, had already reappeared in the 1960s, in their original shades of mauve, olive and murky brown.

The Souleiado museum houses over 40,000 carved fruit-wood blocks, mainly from the eighteenth and nineteenth centuries, offering endless scope to the designers of today. When they are used to build up new designs, the blocks are printed onto translucent acetate, which is then hand-coloured in order to try out new colour combinations. Combining the prints is a fascinating art, requiring both a spirit of adventure and a true appreciation of the intrinsic balance in each design.

Traditional designs, contemporary uses

Nowadays, Provençal patterns have been adapted for weaves and are printed on all types of fabric, from silks and organzas to stretch-cotton Lycra, as well as on the plastic-coated tablecloths that have become so indispensable for young children at table. The Souleiado company was founded on the production of cotton shawls (*mouchoirs*) in three categories: bright coloured designs (*enluminés*) for younger girls and women; discreet grey tones (*grisailles*) for women of a certain age; and dark, muted colours (*deuils*) for old women and those in mourning. Designs for this square format invariably involved a decorative border designed to be compatible with a wide range of different patterns in the centre square. These versatile shawls are still produced, their uses now ranging from the traditional shawl to serving as a small tablecloth or being wrapped over a bikini as a sarong.

The basic idea of a printed border containing a complementary design has proved almost infinitely adaptable. Nowadays it can be seen on all types of bags, on large parasols or smaller umbrellas, on an endless variety of cushions, and on tablecloths in all shapes and colours, complete with matching or contrasting napkins or a mixture of different designs.

The smaller designs lend themselves to gorgeous patchwork prints, with Souleaido's combination of many smaller squares of design put together in one fabric print proving an irresistible temptation to many patchwork enthusiasts. While fashions in both clothes and interiors continue to change and fluctuate, it seems clear that there will always be a place for the small prints of Provençal fabrics, with their talent for mixing and matching, their virtually infinite versatility and their universal appeal.

opposite Souleiado's
pretty patchwork of
their own designs, floral
or paisley, makes an
enchanting baby's quilt.

left A cotton piqué
quilt in a traditional
print. The red of the
background colour
adds cheerful warmth
to a small bedroom,
coordinating naturally
with the Provençal colours
of the floor and walls.

right Traditional costume is still frequently worn by all for festivals, weddings and Christmas celebrations, particularly in the Arles region.

below Small girls frolic around the fountain wearing tiered summer skirts in Provençal prints: not only pretty but also comfortable in the summer heat.

Provençal costume

The Souleiado museum has a collection of Provençal clothing, which not only displays its fabrics but also gives fascinating insights into how people dressed in the past. Women's dress was layered: in summer a light linen blouse with a bustier, and several ankle-length skirts, with a capacious apron over the top, and, underneath, until relatively recently, long and voluminous shorts with an unstitched crutch. In winter, blouses were of wool or fleeced cotton and bustier and skirts were quilted for warmth, with shawls tied over them and a cloak for outdoors. Before the Revolution, most women throughout France wore a white

centre White cotton and linen, cool and crisp, embroidered and beautifully decorated with drawn thread work, once a skill of every country girl.

left Folded linen behind the doors of a traditional *armoire*. The shelves are lined with *indiennes* to provide a smooth, dust-free interior.

bonnet of some kind, although there were different styles. After 1789, their hair was often revealed, in a development considered quite daring among country folk.

The women of Arles

Arlésiennes use their rolled hair as part of their head-dress, a complicated affair built up around a comb and tied in place. The six stages of preparing the hair and the ten stages of securing the tie in place were sketched by local artist Léo Lelée, who also painted women dancing the *farandole*, their costumes a colourful swirl of movement while their hair remains meticulously in place. (These paintings were also reproduced on a dinner service commissioned by Souleiado – see page 66.) Another distinctive feature of this costume is the shawl, which is pinned in pleats over the shoulders to add warmth and to keep it in place. Always fiercely proud of their dress code, many women of Arles can still be seen wearing traditional costume to Sunday Mass, in processions and at other special events.

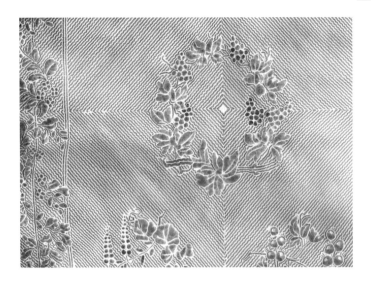

The secret art of *boutis*

Boutis is the traditional needlework quilt of Provence, combining Italian *trapunto* with the quilting technique of running stitch. The finished product is a decorative relief on white cotton and it should never be confused with an ordinary quilt. Unfortunately many shops claim their quilts are traditional *boutis* without understanding the difference. Held up to the light, a true *boutis* is revealed by its translucent quality whereas quilting is opaque.

Each *boutis* design contained a message from its creator: a heart meant 'love'; a flower 'beauty'; an olive twig or perched dove 'peace'; a pineapple 'hospitality'; grapes 'prosperity'; a peacock 'vanity'; a cypress tree 'mourning'; a dove 'peace in death'. The most common symbol was a heart enclosing the initials of those to be married. Wedding clothes were planned years in advance: the bride often wore a long white skirt gathered at the waist, in lightweight quilting or piqué down to the knee with a border of *boutis* descending to the ankle. Some skirts had *boutis* motifs scattered down to the knee, above a thick *boutis* border to the ankle. Most of these beautiful robes are now displayed in museums.

Some women made quilts using the secret language of motifs to tell their life stories. Most *boutis* embroidery, however, is in repeat patterns. Genuine *boutis* quilts command exceptionally high prices and most are now museum pieces. Surviving old examples are often in need of extensive repairs. The tension in the fabric caused by the process of creating relief work was often exacerbated by storage methods. *Boutis* should always be rolled rather than folded, which causes the fabric to split. Provençal museums provide expert advice on repairing *boutis*.

Coloured quilts

A single *boutis* quilt would probably take between seven months and a year to complete, depending on the intricacy of the design, so very few genuine new ones are now to be found. Normal quilts, on the other hand, are to be found in every antique market in teetering piles of aged but colourful Provençal prints. Quilting, or piqué, was traditionally used only for bedroom covers or clothing. Now quilts are used throughout the house, draped over chairs, thrown over tables or tossed over a *radassié* to make a day bed. The most decorative throws are often the older ones, worn a little at the edges, and often with one side still its original deep colour and the other – the side that always lay uppermost on the bed – quite washed out after years of exposure to the sun's rays. Plain

opposite left A true white Provençal *boutis* quilt held up to the light: the raised work is opaque, while the spaces between are translucent like lace.

opposite right
Even chosen at random, Provençal prints have a naturally complementary quality – a stylish and relaxed version of mix and match.

left The most beautiful collection of piqué and patchwork Provençal quilts is on display at the Souleiado museum in Tarascon.

right A quilt lies invitingly over the sofa, adding warmth and softness to a cool architectural interior. The scalloped-edge design is most frequently used in Provence.

opposite A manufactured white quilt is thrown over the bed in a simply furnished room. Shelves built into the thickness of the wall and supported by the plasterwork are typically Provençal.

quilts with a contrasting deep border, and quilts with one print in the centre and a different pattern for a border are just as charming. Manufactured relief quilting can also be purchased by the metre and used in many ways throughout the house, even as upholstery.

Quilting designs

Some simple quilting designs – usually the simplest – are universal, recurring with only minor variations in virtually every culture, but this characteristically Provençal craft also has its own distinctive motifs. They include a corner design of intertwined olive branches with borders of trailing olives; and a central design of eglantine flowers (a symbol of conjugal love) with matching borders, linked with double quilting in squares rather than the habitual diamond.

right Linen makes a
sumptuous tablecloth for
dining *à la belle étoile*.

far right The
farandole is danced
across a plate painted
by Léo Lelée, part of a
dinner service created
for Souleiado.

From flax to linen

Flax germinates in April and is gathered in June (*'c'est juin qui fait le lin'* as the country saying goes) when pretty blue flowers dance over the lush green stalks like swarms of hovering butterflies. Each flower lasts only hours, and when the stalks turn gold, the whole plant is pulled out by the roots to conserve the length of the stem. In the past, flax was cut with a scythe and gathered bunch by bunch and the seedheads, consisting of 30–35 per cent oil from which fine linseed-oil paint is made, removed using large metal combs. The linen stalks were then laid in still water or a gently flowing stream for some weeks while micro-organisms decomposed the tough exterior to leave the strong cellulose fibrous filaments. These were then laid out in the sun to dry and bleach, before being broken down further by an old machine resembling a wooden guillotine which mashed the stalks without cutting them. Finally, the stalks were dragged with a brush of nails, refining the fibres into finer strands. In 1780, an entrepreneur named Philippe de Girard, from Lourmarin, a village not far from Apt, began working

on machinery to simplify this laborious process. After thirty years he succeeded, at which point Protestants fleeing persecution in Lourmarin took the machines with them to Switzerland and Ireland. At the same time a chemist, Claude Louis Berthollet, discovered bleach, and the resulting ability to turn the original dull cream material into white linen laid the foundations of the trade in luxurious, crisp white fabric that continues to this day.

Spinning tales

Making the filaments into linen thread was women's work, though the looms were mainly worked by men. Spinning was done at home on a staff called a *quenouille* which could stand on the ground tucked under the arm of the seated spinner, or be held in her belt while she worked. A small, weighted wooden spindle, called a *fuseau*, was spun in the air with finger and thumb, while the filaments were pulled and moistened with saliva to become the linen thread. As the women sat together spinning, they talked, sang and told stories.

above Each napkin is embroidered with the name of a flower found in Provence.

left An elegant wedding tablecloth designed by Edith Mézard, with a fine linen border in contrasting blue and matching flower napkins.

opposite Edith Mézard at work in the gardens of Château de l'Ange. The workshops can be visited most afternoons.

right Expert hands at work. Edith Mézard embroidering one of her flower napkins.

below right An embroidered 'B' in satin stitch against beige linen.

below Lines from a poem by Jacques Prévert embroidered on a translucent linen curtain.

embroidery

In her studio at Château de l'Ange in the village of Lumières, Edith Mézard continues the linen-working traditions of Provence with an innovative use of traditional and contemporary designs.

Linen is now available in numerous weights, colours and counts (the larger the count, the closer the weave). The finer linens set off embroidery the most attractively: from humble initials on a tea towel to a full set of bed or table linen for a marriage. On the wedding table on the previous page, the embroidery of the napkins reflects the choice of flowers gathered for the occasion from the garden and hedgerows – white jasmine stars, pale lilacs, soft translucent blue plumbago, white roses, deeper violets and waving linen grass, scattered lavender, iris and gardenia.

The wedding napkins are of fine cream linen, embroidered by Edith with the names of the flowers in cream lower-case letters. Each flower name contains within it a pictorial element to signify the flower in question: a petal for one, a slender leaf for another. Each napkin is made from a 53-cm (21-in) wide weave. The selvage edges are naturally hemmed, and the raw edges are pulled into threads to form a fringe. The simplicity of the embroidery and the exceptional quality of the linen together transform an everyday item into an object of considerable elegance.

The white linen tablecloth, bordered with a cobalt-blue linen frame, is mitred over the corners where the two materials join. In Provence, tablecloths, curtains and place mats are often bordered with contrasting fabric, adding interest and making a natural frame. In her more lyrical work, Edith embroiders verses on translucent linen curtains to magical effect – no one can resist a touching line of poetry fluttering in the breeze from an open window. Each curtain bears different lines, often taken from works of the Provençal poet Frédéric Mistral, who did so much to revive the local culture by using the rich Provençal language and writing numerous works on Provence – an achievement for which he received the Nobel prize for literature in 1904.

boutis cushion

Boutis is a term now widely applied to every piece of Provençal printed fabric that has been quilted – to the great dismay of those who know the difference between the two and the amount of work involved. Firstly, with rare exceptions, *boutis* is always white and it is never printed. Secondly, *boutis* consists of two pieces of plain white cotton sewn together with a running stitch that forms the design: the stuffing is then applied strand by strand, passing between the two layers of cotton. The *boutis* method aims not at applying bulk but at creating a beautiful relief, like a structured frieze. *Boutis* was designed first and foremost for decoration, not for warmth. The difference between creating a quilted cushion and a *boutis* cushion is one day's hard work to one week's hard work, which may explain why very few new quilts are made using this technique. The way to ascertain whether an item is of *boutis* or normal quilting is to hold it up to the light. *Boutis* will show transparent lines of stitching with padded forms, whereas quilting is uniformly opaque.

Boutis is beautiful and enjoyable, but be warned and do not count the hours. Beware of reusing the same holes for entry and exit, as they will not close in the first wash. In a well-worked *boutis*, the front and back of the work should be identical once all holes and design marks have been removed by washing. The final edge of the *boutis* should be a row of enclosed thread.

materials and tools
two pieces of plain white cotton fabric, tracing paper and pencil or fabric-washable carbon paper, normal needle, thread, no. 22 tapestry needle, 4-ply cotton thread, embroidery hoop, wooden toothpick or cocktail stick.

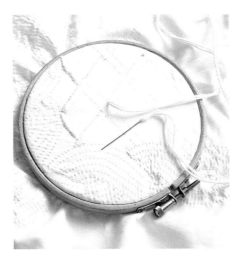

step one Transfer your design onto 1 piece of fabric with tracing paper and pencil or a fabric-washable carbon paper. Loosely tack to the second piece in 10cm (4in) squares. Use a small even running stitch over your pencil lines, working from the centre to avoid distortion or buckling.

step two Double thread a no. 22 tapestry needle with 4-ply cotton thread. Ease it between the 2 layers of an area of the design enclosed by the running stitches, filling it with thread. Do not pull the ends through but leave 25mm (⅞in) clear of the fabric, then cut the thread free.

step three Using a wooden toothpick or cocktail stick, carefully stuff the ends of thread back into the design. Some thicker-line designs will need 2 threads to fill the area, but *boutis* should be full not stiff. When filling leaf and flower motifs, be careful to use the base only once.

quilted bedcover

materials and tools
2 lengths cotton fabric,
wadding,
tracing paper and pencil
or fabric-washable
carbon paper,
needle and thread,
bias binding,
quilting frame if desired.

Take inspiration for your choice of fabrics from both modern and older quilts, always remembering that the soft muted colours of older quilts would originally have been brighter. Cotton fabrics are an ideal choice since they are easy to work and washable. Invest in good quality: this will be reflected in the price but is definitely worthwhile, as investing considerable hours of work in poor materials is always disappointing in the long term. If you are making a double quilt, look for wide fabric or cut the fabric to give a wide centre panel with two narrow panels on the sides. Wadding for quilts is available in varying thicknesses, from very thick to thin if you choose polyester, or even thinner in a new, very warm product called Thermolam, which is useful for achieving warmth without bulk.

Many books insist you should use a frame for quilting, but this will depend on where and how you work. Frames do not suit me personally, as I tend to move around the house when quilting. Even for a double quilt I simply tacked the three layers of work together before beginning the running stitches. To avoid buckling when working on a double quilt, it is a good idea to clear the floor, so that you can spread the materials out. Try to avoid using pins when quilting, as they can be very elusive but equally painful when found later. This is a lengthy project, but the end result is splendid and will last a lifetime, and hand-stitched quilts are handed down from generation to generation in many families.

step one Transfer your design onto 1 length of plain fabric, using tracing paper and pencil or fabric-washable carbon paper, obtainable from specialist needlework shops.

step two Sandwich wadding between the two fabrics, and tack into 10cm (4in) squares. Use a small, even running stitche over the design lines, working from the centre out.

step three Remove tacking and enclose the raw edges, either by turning them in and blind-hemming them, or by adding bias binding to render the work durable.

Furniture typical of the Provençal style is readily identifiable by the voluptuous, generous movement of its lines and decorative details, betraying the indelible influence of the Louis XV and Louis XVI styles of the eighteenth century. Curved backs and bow fronts are beautifully carved and embellished in sumptuous woods, including mulberry, golden walnut, cherry, pear and willow. The grandest pieces were often made for a particular occasion. Imposing wardrobes (*armoires*) were frequently part of the marriage dowry, and would be carved with the date, the couples initials and appropriate motifs: intertwined hearts and kissing doves for love, sheaves of wheat for prosperity, vines for longevity and olive branches in abundance. Moulded edging lent panels set into the doors and sides a wonderful sense of movement. Provence also boasts several intriguing types of furniture specific to the region, including the *panetière* for keeping bread and the rush-seated banquette.

furniture

opposite Florid movement accentuated by carved moulding. The fine grille protects the books from insects.
above An exceptional carved *armoire* – the crown indicates it was made for a noble client.

right The stone fireplace was the focus of life, particularly during the winter months. Here water was heated, meals were cooked, clothes were dried and hams were smoked. The unusual vaulted ceiling is supported by impressively large beams, darkened by smoke.

opposite A charming painted chair in eighteenth-century style, positioned invitingly by a half-open window. The painted screen is reminiscent of the naïve nineteenth-century mural paintings of landscapes that used to decorate many Provençal houses.

Most fireplaces in traditional Provençal houses are hewn from massive blocks of local stone. In smaller homes they can seem disproportionately large, constructed as they were at a period when adequate space for cooking, for warming large cauldrons of water and for drying laundry was still an essential requirement. In this way, an entire wall in the kitchen was often taken up with the fireplace, and as the years passed the lofty mantelpiece remained, while electric cookers and gas hobs were accommodated beneath in a natural marriage of old and new requirements. In larger properties, the stone chimneypiece usually continued up to the ceiling, offering the opportunity for an additional panel of stone carving or moulded detail.

right The exuberant pharmacy in the eighteenth-century Hôtel Dieu in Carpentras.

Extra storage space is always welcome and a good Provençal never abandons a door. There are even antique shops specializing in doors alone. Smaller doors are set in plaster frames and used for cupboards, while whole wardrobe fronts may be recessed into exceptionally thick supporting walls. Plaster has many uses in Provence, where it serves to make shelf supports, kitchen units, little alcoves and even banisters.

Painted furniture

Furniture was often painted, particularly that made from pale wood such as beech. The strong Provençal light encourages both pale and bold colour combinations, and popular decorative schemes are based on fruit and flowers, sometimes with local pastoral scenes. Styles are as varied as the artists' talents, and the patina of age adds extra charm. Most of today's painted furniture aims to mimic this patina through a process of painting and sanding in varying colours, building up the effect of years with weeks of painting. Originally painted finishes were usually used to disguise inexpensive wood, and were robust and flamboyant in style, like the Hôtel Dieu pharmacy in Carpentras. Here ochre and deep blue paintwork sets up rich contrasts, with each drawer intriguingly labelled with the name of an eighteenth-century remedy. Pastoral scenes decorate the lower panels, while cherubs wait in the heavens should the medicine fail to work!

Traditional types

Traditional Provençal furniture includes the *commode*, or chest of drawers, and the *buffet*, or sideboard, with doors. Both are almost invariably carved, and some sit on curving legs with sculpted rolled feet known as *escargots*, or snails. A typical addition to the *buffet* is a low plate cupboard with sliding doors.

right The curvaceous lines of a typically Provençal *commode*.

centre The appeal of a simple and sturdy *buffet* in Bruno Carles' entrance hall is enhanced by its distressed paint finish, bearing all the hallmarks of age.

opposite Jacotte Vagh's solid butcher's block has seen generations of wear.

Pétrins and panetières

The *panetière* is a small and highly decorative cupboard with a solid door flanked by open storage space barred with turned spindles, and extremely solid hinges and key. Used to keep baked bread, it was hung on the wall to escape rodents while the open bars allowed the air to circulate. The large lock, meanwhile, was to stop thieving fingers. Beneath the *panetière* stood the *pétrin*, an equally decorative airtight trough with a lid, used to store the rising dough. Frequently the two pieces would have been made as a matching pair by the same carpenter, but sadly most have now been separated.

Two charming wooden boxes resembling miniature wardrobes set on tiny feet are also typically Provençal pieces. One, with a sloping top and a little drawer placed at the bottom, is the *salière*, where salt was kept in bulk, while the drawer was used for storing spices. The other is the *farinière*, used to store flour. When this ingenious piece was laid on its back, the sliding panel door could

be opened so that a fish could be coated with flour: hence the fish decoration often carved on this sliding panel.

Tables were simpler on the whole, with either straight, tapering legs or a deep, undulating panel that hid the silverware drawers, balanced on beautifully curvaceous legs finished off with dainty doe's feet, known as *pieds de biche*. Later examples might have sliding panels or a double top, which rotates and opens out to extend the table area and accommodate larger gatherings. Much of this Provençal furniture, and particularly the wardrobes, was highly embellished with lovely iron or steel fretwork *ferrures*, placed round locks for both decoration and security. Some *ferrures* are quite beautiful and have survived on the furniture over the years.

right Symmetrically arranged *ferrures* are a characteristic adornment of Provençal furniture.

centre Dainty and delicate though they may appear, *ferrures* serve the unromantic function of adding strength to the lock.

opposite An elegant polished steel *ferrure* mounted on a beautifully inlaid fruitwood drawer.

Centres of production

The main furniture-producing area in Provence was historically the Rhône valley, which offered easy transportation down river from Valence, Montélimar, Orange and Avignon and into the Mediterranean from Vallabrègues, Tarascon and Arles. Merchants traded their wares down the Rhône, so avoiding the mountains. The river also supplied many of the essential elements of furniture production. The fruit trees, willows and reeds that grew along the long and fertile river banks supplied not only carpenters and carvers, but also chair-cane weavers and basket makers. Local towns grew prosperous, particularly Arles, which developed an unrivalled reputation for exceptional furniture and elaborate carving. The Rhône valley still boasts many excellent craftsmen, and while many of the arduous tasks are now assisted by electric machinery, most of the work involved in assembly, carving and painting has not changed significantly for generations.

Easily recognizable differences in style can be attributed originally to religious differences. The Protestants sheltering in the wild, rocky landscape of Haute Provence produced restrained pieces with more straight lines and geometric decoration than curves. In the Basse Provence to the south, Catholic craftsmen – catering to a wealthier clientele – indulged in billowing, voluptuous forms and extravagantly detailed decoration. Both camps produced the range of typical pieces but in strikingly different fashion.

In his antique and furniture shop in the Camargue, Bruno Carles notices the difference immediately. The family antiques firm gave Bruno a sound education in style, and he is inspired by old designs to create new models, which he sells alongside established antiques. His designs are classics and beautifully produced, no longer made in traditional willow, but in beech and less expensive pine, which, when subtly painted with rabbit-skin size, pigment and a few secret ingredients, acquire the soft tones of old furniture.

Exotic woods

The early eighteenth-century boom in shipbuilding in Marseille, Toulon and La Ciotat led to massive deforestation of the wooded uplands of Provence, such as Mont Ventoux. However, the opening of the Suez Canal in 1869, and the resulting access to the Far East, combined with the French colonization of Algeria, catapulted Marseille to the position of France's premier port. Among its imports was a range of new and exotic woods. When resting between boats, Marseille's shipwrights turned their exceptional skills to furniture commissions, making full use of these newly imported woods to add to the wealth and diversity of Provençal furniture. It is still possible to find rare wardrobes with highly polished panels in exotic woods, and others decorated with the highly intricate carving that is only possible in the harder, more exotic species of wood.

Seat furniture

Many newly produced chairs are available throughout Provence, as old chairs tend to be too fragile for daily use. Chairs were traditionally made from a combination of woods: mulberry for the sides, legs and stretchers, since the wood is resistant to woodworm and hard enough for detailed carving; and more flexible beech for the back supports. The typical three-seater *banquette*, or *radassié* (a *radasse* was a lady of easy virtue), traditionally stands in front of the fire, flanked by deep high-backed armchairs. The most capacious of these are called *fauteuils à la bonne femme* and were designed to accommodate ladies of advanced years.

Rush-seated chairs: a versatile classic

Rush-seated chairs are not always comfortable, particularly the flat-backed versions, many of which bear the tell-tale marks of upholstery nails once used to attach horsehair pads. Most rush

opposite left
A country chair and longcase clock have a refined simplicity and natural elegance.

opposite right
A humble all-purpose cupboard – possibly used to store grain as well as linen – softly painted in cream with a red trim.

left A modern chair by Bruno Carles, made using time-honoured techniques. Plump cushions provide added comfort.

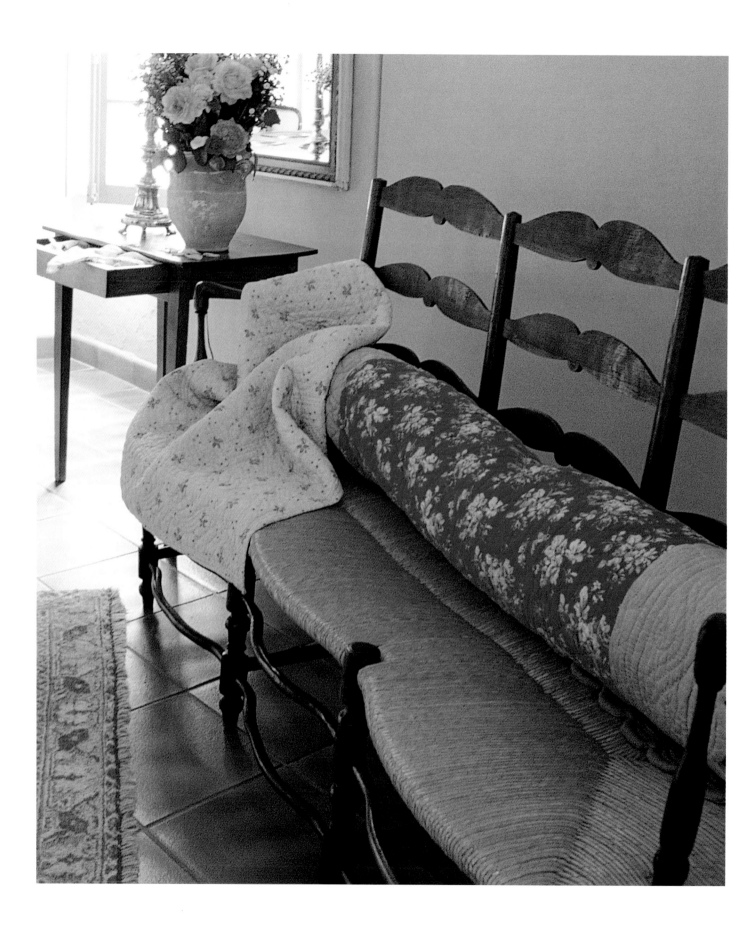

seating is natural in colour, though sometimes the rushes were dyed in order to obtain a coloured pattern.

With curved backs and added cushions, the chairs can be both supportive and comfortable. *Chaises de nourrice* for nursing mothers were also placed by the fire, with a high back for maximum comfort, a low seat for an extended lap, and arms to support the mother's arm as she cradles the baby's head. In the kitchen there would be a low chair without arms, used for changing the baby on the lap. These were also useful for people working by hand who required an unencumbered lap for embroidery, basket making or other crafts.

Additional stretchers bracing the bottom of the legs give extra strength and provide an opportunity for more carved detail. Glue was not used on most older Provençal chairs, which were held together instead by the perfect fit of the finely turned components of their structure.

The support of solid rush seating and the weight of the seated person combined to lock the chair together. Older chairs tend to creak and rock when tentatively tested in antique shops, but may be perfectly solid when you actually sit on them.

Simpler, more rustic chairs do not have the added refinement of a *cache-paille*: a carved wooden band designed to hide and protect the underside of the rush seating. *Cache-pailles* may be delicately carved or beautifully hand-painted. Frequently they mimic the form and decoration of the back support and in antique pieces they may retain more details of the original workmanship as they have been subject to less punishing wear over the years.

The Monleau family, furniture makers of Vallabrègues, have adapted their chair patterns over the course of five generations with comfort very much in mind. The current designs range from miniature chairs for very young children to the traditional and generous *fautenils à la bonne femme* created for grandmothers, and the chair for which the Monleau family is famous.

opposite An invitingly curvaceous *radassié*, draped with quilts.

left Outline detail picked out in contrasting paint adds definition to the paintwork.

below Another example of a Bruno Carles chair. Note the softly curved lines of the stretchers and the pretty detail of the *cache-paille*, designed to conceal and protect the rush seating.

above The well-used glue pot of the Monleau family business.

above right Virginie begins to apply the first weaves of the rush seating.

chair making

In the second week of August each year, the small town of Vallabrègues on the Rhône celebrates its past glory as a centre of basket weaving and chair making. Carts are piled high with baskets for the autumn fruit harvest, while rush weavers and furniture makers fill the narrow streets with their wares. It was here that the famous Van Gogh chair was made by the great-grandfather of the Monleau family, furniture makers in Vallabrègues to this day.

Women stop by on the way to market to see when their skills are required, and take the chairs home with them to cane them at their open doors. A simple rush-seated chair takes up to four hours to complete and a three-seater *radassié* takes a whole day. The painted chair frame is anchored to a weighted base – often a lump of concrete on a support pole. Tension is applied while the outer rush layer is twisted over the supporting strong raffia base. The smaller the chair, the easier the work, and nowadays few people have the necessary skill and strength to complete the whole of a *radassié* seat in one continuous weave, as tradition demands.

left Hanging against the wall are templates for the many different models of chair that Monleau has produced over the last four generations.

below Ellen, full of charm, assembles the chairs and welcomes clients' interest.

painted three-seater

Chairs in Provence may be painted in any shade of ochre, from the blood-red found only in Roussillon to the deep mustards or sandy yellows of other parts of Provence, with parts of the turned legs picked out in a contrasting colour. Soft sage green or faded off-white are also favourites and make subtle backgrounds for painted designs. The paints traditionally used would have been made from a mixture of ground natural pigments and rabbit-skin sizes, very gently applied to give a rich, smooth depth of colour. As rabbit-skin size contains protein, it goes off very quickly in the heat, so I must admit to cheating by using oil paint mixed with a little poppy oil, which adds gloss while also thinning down the paint. But there can be no comparison between a chair lovingly painted with up to twenty coats of rabbit-skin size and pigment and one painted with a mere four layers of artist's oils.

Flowers and fruits are the inspiration for most decorative carving and painting, though dates, places and names may also figure. Each chair back can be different, perhaps featuring the same plant at different times of the year. The olive flowers in May, for instance, then produces green fruits, which turn black in chilly December; add a spray of leaves or a few olives and you have a charming design. Mask off all rush seating, then start painting, using a mixture of diluted artist's quality oils and alkyd flow medium, checking that all areas are covered. Leave to dry thoroughly, then sand with fine sandpaper and repeat the process twice.

materials and tools
masking tape,
artist's quality oil paints,
poppy oil,
alkyd flow medium
(for consistency over
raw wood),
tracing paper and pencil,
paintbrushes – a square-
edged 25mm
(1in) for larger surfaces
and a 12mm (½in) for
detail on chair legs,
round brushes sizes 4–7
for motif,
fine sandpaper.

step one After painting the whole chair as outlined above, position your traced design over the chair back and attach it with masking tape. Transfer it onto the chair and mark with pencil any lines that seem faint.

step two Paint in a base of pale green on your design (here Monestial blue combined with lemon yellow), using the pencil markings as a guide. Add a little poppy oil to the oil paint to thin it and add sheen.

step three Finally, paint in the details. Monestial blue and crimson alizarine together make deep purple/black for the olives. Add touches of blue to the leaf sides and some crimson alizarine to the stems.

fabric-covered café chairs

materials and tools
tape measure,
2m (6½ ft) x 90cm (35in)
upholstery fabric,
sewing machine,
needle and thread,
scissors and pins.

These chair covers are ideal for creating versatile seating, both indoors and out. Chosen to coordinate with your interior, they allow you quickly to wipe a folding garden chair and bring it inside as the need arises. In the summer, garden chairs can be clothed in elegant Provençal fabrics for a more formal outdoor gathering. This choice of varying checks in different colours offers plenty of scope both indoors and out. Use the remnants to make small cushions that fit snugly into the hollow of the back. The Tarascon factory that produced the materials used here respects centuries-old traditions, in which the fabrics are tightly woven by hand, then painted with vegetable dyes. They have appeared as the favourite faded shirts of Picasso, and also grace the shelves of Fifth Avenue stores.

When choosing your fabric, make sure it has enough weight to hang properly, but is not too difficult to iron. Since these covers are not stretched over a frame, they tend to crease if you use a fabric that is too lightweight. Before cutting out your material, you need to take some basic measurements. For the main panel, measure from the floor, up to and across the seat, up the back and down to the floor again for the length, and from side to side for the width. For the two side panels, measure the depth of the seat for the width and from seat to floor for the length. Typical measurements for a chair cover will give a main panel of 2m x 50cm (6½ ft x 20 in) and two side panels of 47 x 40cm (19 x 16in).

step one Cut out the panels, then turn back and hem the top and bottom edges. To make the ties, cut 16 strips of fabric, 4 x 25cm (1½ x 10in). Fold the raw side edges under and machine-stitch carefully down each strip.

step two Turn over the sides of the main seat panel to fold in the raw edges. Enclose the ribbon ties in the rolled edges at convenient points and pin. Repeat this procedure for the two side panels.

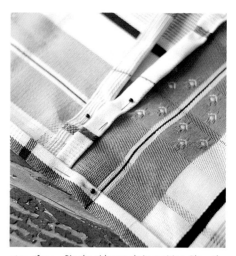

step three Pin the side panels in position. Place the cover over the chair and check that the side panels are correctly positioned and that the ribbon ties on the main and side panels correspond. Machine-stitch in place.

Metalwork in Provence epitomizes that magical contrast between the inherent strength of the material used and the breathtaking delicacy with which it can be worked. Everywhere you look, you see evidence of the *ferronnier*'s craft: long graceful balconies are *de rigueur* on many houses, airy wrought-iron campaniles crown old churches and metal silhouette signs swing above shops. Massive wooden doors are embellished with intricate cast-iron work and moulded door-knockers; filigree gates protect larger *domaines*, while *porte-fenêtres*, those elegant tall windows that allow the light to flood into upper storeys, are embellished by lacy wrought-iron balustrades. In gardens, used year round for eating and socializing, chairs and tables are often metal: heavy enough to withstand the mistral wind, but also irresistibly attractive with their traditional curved designs. Welcome shade is, meanwhile, likely to be provided by vine-laden iron trelliswork. **metalwork**

opposite Bruno Carles's distinctive 'green' chairs display to perfection the graceful arabesques of the backs and the decorative punched-metal seats. **above** A typical door-knocker.

right A romantic pergola, twisted with age, provides support for young climbers, planted to give shade in years to come. A candelabrum adds a flamboyant touch on summer evenings.

opposite A broad expanse of simple trelliswork, covered with wisteria, shades a beautiful sunken terrace.

below An exceptional wrought-iron chair from Bruno Carles's collection of antique garden furniture.

Garden furniture

Traditional metal garden chairs have backs in the form of a heart motif in wrought iron with a punched-metal seat, or combine a very comfortable curvaceous wrought-iron back with a seat in open meshwork. Open punched work, used for both seats and table tops, is not only attractive in its lightness of design, but is also very practical, preventing water from collecting and thus promoting the inevitable rusting. Many of the older, more traditional designs are now being reproduced in large factories using moulds and automation. Each new chair is still assembled by hand, however, so they retain their original charm.

Older wrought-iron chairs and tables can still be found in village shops and antique markets. In his antique shop, Bruno Carles has a collection that he has rescued from a rusty grave and lovingly restored to a smooth finish. The table top is always the first element to scratch and rust, with the layers of paint peeling and blistering over the years. As an alternative to repainting, the metalwork can instead be sprayed with a matt varnish, which prevents further rusting while retaining the patina of age.

Most metal chairs tend to be upright, but lower designs upholstered with sprung metal bands are now collectors' items, prized for their sculptural charm. Bruno has a varied collection of these surprisingly comfortable round-seated chairs in stock.

Pergolas and trellises

Wrought-iron metal pergolas, hexagonal, octagonal or circular, provide a romantic support for wisteria, roses or jasmine, which twine round them to form a natural scented canopy of flowers in season and cast dappled shade throughout the summer.

Curvaceous trellises, meanwhile, are supported against sunny walls, throwing a soothing mottled shade over the terrace and providing support for flowering climbers and vines heavily laden with grapes. These leaning arbours, or *treilles*, act as a natural filter to the sun as it streams through the large windows on the

south side of the house, away from the mistral wind. Some trellises are highly ornate, with curves and flourishes topped with pine-cone finials, while others opt for the simplicity and restraint found in plain arching metalwork. When designing from new, it is tempting, with the encouragement of the *ferronnier*, to favour very ornate forms of trelliswork, but attention should ultimately focus on the movement of the climbing stems. They will soon dominate the scene, beautiful both in their gaunt winter state and resplendent in summer flower.

Balconies and balustrades

Ornate wrought-iron balconies bearing coats of arms grace the mansions lining the Cours Mirabeau in Aix, Provence's former capital. Smaller balconies perch prettily above narrow cobbled alleys in every village, some ornately curved and decorated, others plain and simple in design with straight bars or, as is typically Provençal, one straight vertical bar alternating with a twisted or 'wiggle' bar.

In many villages, especially those enclosed within thick fortified walls, gardens are a rarity, so balconies provide precious outdoor space and serve as an extension to the room within, allowing the owner to catch the midday sun or to overhear the neighbours' gossip. Many taller windows have a wrought-iron balustrade for safety, and the theme is often continued around the house, even on smaller windows. Equally decorative yet functional are the generously bowed wrought-iron grilles that provide security to ground-floor windows.

While it is tempting to consider crime a modern problem, the thickness of seventeenth-century window bars indicates otherwise. Originally waxed, these bars are now protected with clear anti-rust paint. Superb examples may be seen on the lower windows of the *hôtels particuliers* on the south side of the Cours Mirabeau in Aix. Now mainly converted into banks, they may easily be visited to admire their sweeping stairs lined with intricate wrought-iron banisters as well as their wonderful balconies.

The oval 'bull's-eye' windows found in roofs and upper storeys throughout France have distinctive variations in Provence where they are also found in diamond, rectangular, circular and square form. All are protected, however, by a strong iron bar, which is slashed, peeled back and hammered out to form an 'ear of wheat', which affords security while allowing light to enter a loft or brighten the area near a front door. Bull's-eye windows also once gave an unobtrusive view of approaching attack; today they are useful for keeping an eye on children at play.

opposite left
A bull's-eye window
protected by a forged
metal bar, slashed
to resemble an ear
of wheat.

opposite centre
Swooping bars and
forged scrollwork render
a window decorative
but impregnable.

opposite right
A *porte-fenêtre* with a
wrought-iron balustrade
in an unusual design.

left Small and simple,
a balcony stocked
with petunias and
pelargoniums, and
complemented by
peeling shutters,
seems to encapsulate
the charm of Provence.

Gates and shutters

While ornate wrought-iron is both attractive and effective, typically heavy shutters are an even more serious deterrent. They are made of a double thickness of tongue-and-groove wood, arranged vertically on the inside and horizontally on the exterior. The two thicknesses are nailed together with large and very long flat-headed nails, forged specially for the purpose. These are hammered through from the inside of the shutter and then bent over and hammered back through again, rendering the shutters virtually impregnable. Older shutters often have a sliding peephole through which to look out while the shutters are closed. On the author's house, this sliding shutter overlooks the main drive, and is just big enough to shoot game through. It was last used in living memory to fire grapeshot at an American GI as he helped himself to a chicken.

To confuse invaders in earlier centuries and nowadays to protect privacy, entrances were unobtrusively set back within thick walls and fortified by strong wrought-iron gates that filled the opening, often embellished with crests or trade signs. Barricades have remained a defence not only against civil strife and foreign invasion, but also against the bearers of disease. The gateway ports of the Mediterranean – Marseille, Toulon and Arles – were all struck by the plague in the fifteenth century and half the population of Marseille perished in the great plague of 1720. In 1883 a cholera epidemic brought more fear and panic in its wake. And to cap it all, religious minorities such as the Jewish and Protestant communities might at any time find themselves the victims of persecution.

Architectural salvage companies sell both gates and supporting pillars, but it is worth comparing prices, here and in antique shops, with the cost of commissioning the local *ferronnier*, who will often prove less expensive. Leave new gates untreated so that they rust, then paint them with a clear anti-rust solution to achieve a charming aged effect.

opposite left
Graceful movement in metalwork strengthens a front door.

opposite centre
The two thicknesses of wood making up a shutter are clearly revealed as the top layer flakes away with age.

opposite right
A classic cast-iron door-knocker in the form of a woman's hand.

left Part of the original defensive wall is virtually all that remains of the fourteenth-century fortress of the Avignon popes that gave Châteauneuf-du-Pape its name. Modern wrought iron now fills a gateway.

far right The ornate bell tower in Aix has two levels for looking over the town square or out into the hills.

right A highly wrought campanile has complementary finials and elaborate balustrades.

Campaniles and shop signs

Throughout Provence, wrought-iron bell towers or campaniles dominate the skyline, from the highly ornate bell tower of the Hôtel de Ville in Aix to the starkly simple pyramidal campanile of Rousset-sur-Arc in the Var. Wrought-iron campaniles date mainly from the nineteenth century when they were placed on churches, town gates and municipal buildings.

The campanile at Eyguières, Bouches-du-Rhône, is perfectly cylindrical, another at Les Pennes-Mirabeau is hexagonal, looking rather like a pergola, while the one in Apt is completely square. Le Thor in the Vaucluse and Manosque boast exotic constructions in the form of a light bulb, while Toulon in the Var and Le Luc both have tiered crowns. A weather vane was an important adjunct to traditional campaniles, usually in the form of a flag or cross with an arrow beneath giving the wind direction. The bells, meanwhile, tolled the hour, church services and festivals, but most importantly they pealed out forest fire warnings. Unimpeded by brick casements, they could be heard for miles. Many bell towers were the highest point in the village and served as watchtowers for forest fires. During times of drought, when the strong winds could fan the flames quickly into a wall of fire, there was very little communities could do apart from hope to have adequate warning to release their livestock and run.

Metal shop signs are an attractive feature of many Provençal villages and continue a long-held tradition of advertising based on symbols. The tradition goes back to Roman times, and before the spread of literacy signs were invaluable aids to identifying the premises of different shops and warehouses. Silhouette signs cut out of metal hung over every tradesman's entrance, craftsman's workshop and doctor's and lawyer's offices alike.

left A cryptic owl
demonstrates the
whimsical side of the
ferronnier's craft.

above A classic
example of a silhouette
shop sign, showing
a nineteenth-century
horsewoman on her
prancing steed.

Wrought-iron beds

Strong, durable and decorative, wrought-iron beds are also less expensive than their much-prized wooden cousins. They were produced in small factories from 1850 onwards, with the corners invariably embellished with identical decorative swirls. The various parts were secured with rounded metal clips, the only soldering being for the cup in which the side of the bed fits to stabilize the foot and head. Easily repaired, they are cunning in design, as both sides of the bed unclip to fold flat over the bed base. The head and foot of the bed then pivot flat over the sides and base to make an ingeniously compact little package.

Many of these beds owe their existence today to their ease of storage and are now being rescued from attics and cellars where they had taken up very little space.

Metal beds are simple to restore, whether by professionally sand blasting to a gunmetal finish and spray painting, or by simply rubbing down with wire wool and finishing off with natural wax, giving an aged but not rusty look.

A matching pair of these beds, from a batch commissioned by a local convent, proved to be a generous 140cm (56in) wide – large enough for the largest of nuns. Children's cots, made to the same design, also fold flat and are easily stored.

Delightful cots, miniature beds and swinging cribs can be found in many antique markets today, but do bear in mind that although they may have been used safely for generations, the bars are often wide enough apart for a small child to wriggle through and even get stuck.

metal through which the smoke escaped. One of the glass sides was a door, with a large loop for the simple sliding bolt. The lamplighter slipped his long staff through the loop to open the glass door, lit the wick and closed the door again. In lamps adapted for gas, the door remained but an incandescent gas mantle replaced the brass container with taper, and a white enamel disc was inserted into the funnel interior to refract the light. Many lamps converted to electricity are thus now on their third incarnation, demonstrating the solid design of the original lamp and the durability of the *ferronnier*'s art.

Lamps may be either suspended from above or supported from underneath on a decorative set of four to six stable curved prongs, usually square or hexagonal in shape. Whether suspending or supporting a lamp, this metal support is known as a console. Consoles vary in form from place to place, according to the local *ferronnier*'s preferred designs. It was essential that they should be strong, as the lanterns were normally large – some as big as 65cm (26in) high by 35cm (14in) across the widest part of the funnel – and in the days when they were powered by oil or gas were considerably heavier than modern versions lit by electricity. Lanterns hang on the side of buildings, so keeping the street clear for pedestrians, or are strung between ancient plane trees, filling village squares with a nocturnal glow.

Additional lighting for both the house and garden is made by the *ferronnier*. Metalwork candelabra are popular in Provence, lighting alfresco summer dining tables or subtle candlelit evenings around the winter fire. There are many different classic designs to choose from, and as with all wrought ironwork it can be well worth while to work with the local *ferronnier* to produce an original contemporary model. The craft of the *ferronier* is alive and well in modern Provence, producing witty and inventive takes on classic features such as lamps and sundials, and making full use of the versatility of wrought iron and other metals, which seem to blend so happily with other local materials.

Lanterns and candelabra

Further evidence of the tradition of wrought iron in Provence can be found in the region's numerous hanging street lamps. Lit initially by means of a combustible liquid and taper, they were then transformed into hissing gas lamps and many were finally converted to electricity. Originally, they consisted of a metal frame with glass sides and a fixed base, and a funnel top of finer sheet

opposite A classic design for a suspended console supporting a lantern has stood the test of time.

left Original and fun, a contemporary lizard sundial is full of charm and shows off the skill of the *ferronnier*.

far left A typical *nasse* trap for snails made from wire.

centre A modern hanging basket acting both as fruit basket and chandelier.

left A *fil-de-fer* salad dryer (displaying eggs). The top closed over the lettuce so you could go outside and rotate your arm vigorously to dry the leaves.

Fil-de-fer

Traditional throughout central Europe, the venerable craft of wirework has accompanied the endless migration of peoples throughout the Mediterranean. In Provence, *fil-de-fer* work ranges from the interlaced wire repair completed on a prized earthenware pot to complicated and highly decorative tiered fruit baskets or hanging candelabra. The inexpensive wire threads are available in many sizes and in copper as well as iron, and simple shapes can be made over an existing earthenware bowl or humble flowerpot.

Wirework skills were traditionally equally valuable inside and outside the house. Rodent traps and little round coops to protect young chicks were made by wrapping chicken wire over a firmer wire support. Sturdy wire baskets were universally useful, and open wire baskets with sturdy wooden handles were used to bring logs into the house. Long, tall, fat, thin or stout, wire holders and containers were made for every conceivable purpose. Economical and attractive, with a functional, stylish appeal, they remain equally popular today.

Within the home, baskets may be extremely decorative: tiered hanging baskets overflowing with seasonal fruits; trays with pretty open-loop wire; small scallop-edged containers with pretty, lifting handles – all are irresistible. And no Provençal kitchen would be complete without its lettuce shaker-cum-egg basket.

Birdcages and tailor's dummies

Personal favourites in *fil-de-fer* are extravagant birdcages fashioned around a light wooden frame, the wooden base acting as a stable foundation for the vertical wires that pierce the first storey and continue through the second to be secured in the roof. Some are constructed like casinos, others like mosques, while yet others boast little folly towers and steeply sloping roofs. Some of these cages are magical, and can make delightful ornamental features, with or without a resident bird.

Another favourite is the old-fashioned tailor's dummy that can be adapted for your own dressmaking – the perfect dummy for your fitting of course being your own figure.

blacksmith
The blacksmith's skill and tools have not changed for centuries, although pollution control measures mean that open furnaces are no longer permitted in built-up areas. The two ends of the anvil, one a rounded 'beak' and the other a tapering square, allow the blacksmith to hammer the red-hot metal rod into shape using both the shape of the anvil and the force of the blows. The anvil sits on a block of wood to absorb the impact of continual hammering: the hammer must never strike the anvil directly or it could split.

Pre-moulded pieces are now available and, although shunned by purists, they allow more options when designing a gate or banister. Worked curves and arabesques hammered over the anvil can now be combined with pre-moulded finials for a tenth of the price a blacksmith would charge. To give an example, a gate with 40 *fleur-de-lis* finials would be prohibitively expensive made from scratch. Instead, find a blacksmith, give him a sketch and the pre-moulded finials and experiment with different possibilities. Spacing out metal rods on the floor and judging proportions, mixing and matching metal pattern pieces, adding and taking away pre-moulded elements in order to assess the initial design idea, reversing the designs, as wrought ironwork is rarely seen just from one side: the whole process is fascinating. A banister bought from architectural salvage provided another challenge to the blacksmith: parts had to be removed and repositioned at the correct angle to the stair drop, and a simple element of the design copied to fill in missing links. To integrate the new soldering, the whole banister was stippled with greasy black metal-stove paint and polished with dusting cloths. This protects the iron from further rust while providing a soft mottled black finish to the completed rail.

opposite above
Elements of the 'sleeping dog' motif so characteristic of Provence.

opposite below
The tools of the trade. The type and weight of the hammer is matched to the metal used and the shape required.

centre Hammered out over the anvil, an iron strip is transformed into a graceful curve.

left A combination of wrought-iron hammered on the anvil and pre-moulded pieces, viewed from behind.

punched metal food cupboard

Small cheese safes are easy to make. They should be light and transportable and, most important of all, have enough holes to allow good air circulation – but not so big that they allow tiny flies and insects to penetrate. Makers and sellers of cheese throughout France are adamant about one thing: do not keep cheese in the fridge, as you destroy its delicate flavours and inhibit it from maturing naturally. Instead, cheese should be wrapped in paper and kept in a cool, airy cheese cupboard.

The idea of this project is to repair or adapt a small food cupboard to make a cheese safe, replacing the existing solid front panel with one of punched metal, a treatment that has been used since the eighteenth century as a practical means of keeping insects at bay and the cheese within cool and aired. The holes would have been pierced with the rough side out, but it is safer to expose the smooth side on the front of the cupboard. Fine metal mesh is available from hardware shops, as is aluminium or tin-plated sheet steel. Aluminium 22-gauge is better suited to a smaller project; tin-plated sheet steel 28-gauge can be used for larger projects, but it is tougher and therefore harder to work. When perforating this stronger metal, turn it over to check the depth of the perforations, as it requires a little practice to apply the same hammer strike each time. With thinner metal, use a pin. When you have finished the panel, nail or staple it to the inside of the cupboard door with the smooth side to the front. If necessary, cover the rough metal edges inside the cupboard with wooden battens for extra protection.

materials and tools
1 small food cupboard –
free-standing,
aluminium 22-gauge
sheet steel for smaller
projects or tin-plated
sheet steel 28-gauge for
larger projects,
paint, pencil,
masking tape,
wooden battens,
sandpaper,
paintbrush,
tool for cutting metal,
nail and hammer or pin.

step one Remove the existing panel from the door and cut a sheet of metal to slightly overlap it in size. Wear gloves and be careful of the cut metal edges. If desired, sand the cupboard and paint it.

step two Either draw a free-hand design or use photocopies to scale up a smaller design. Geometric or stylized designs work well. Centre the design over the sheet of metal and secure it with masking tape.

step three Place the metal on a piece of waste wood and push a pin or hammer a nail through at regular intervals, leaving space between the holes so the design does not pull out like perforated paper.

decorative wire surround

materials and tools
glass or ceramic dish,
wire mesh,
length of galvanized
wire and some very fine
wire for 'sewing',
old pair of scissors,
screwdriver or spoon,
pliers,
spray paint or oven
cleaner spray

Durable, inexpensive and flexible, wire can be used for both ornamental and practical designs, to create anything from baskets and wine-bottle holders to elegant chandeliers. Plain wire and chicken wire are readily available, wire coat hangers can be saved and used for strength, and galvanized wire comes in varying thicknesses from very fine upwards. One of the easiest forms to create is a basket made of plain wire, using a flowerpot as a mould. Circles of wire round the top and bottom of the pot are linked together with four or more vertical wire supports, which can be finished off to act as feet. Wire mesh or strands of coloured wire can then be wrapped around the whole structure to achieve the desired result.

In the project shown here, thin wire mesh has been moulded round a more complex shape (an inverted glass dessert bowl) to produce a decorative surround for a large candle standing in its own dish. You can use any shape you wish as a mould, but the easiest surfaces to work with are glass or ceramic. The wire mesh is manipulated easily into shape and held firm by hoops of stronger, galvanized wire at the base and the top. For greater emphasis of design and increased stability, extra hoops can be inserted, as shown here at the base. Once removed from the chosen mould, the mesh can either be left plain or spray painted, or even, to give it a distressed look, sprayed with oven cleaner.

step one Measure two-thirds of the circumference of the chosen object and cut a piece of mesh that width with an old pair of scissors. Fold about 5cm (2in) up and under the base, then stretch the mesh to its fullest extent to make up the remaining third.

step two Mould the mesh to the object, massaging it into the shape until it fits snugly against the surface of the object. To accentuate any grooves or indentations, use a thin blunt/rounded tool (such as a screwdriver or spoon) to deepen and define the grooves.

step three Measure the base circumference and make a circle of galvanized wire, using pliers to link the ends together. Carefully open up the mesh to remove object, then tilt on side to insert hoop. Make a similar hoop for the top and sew up the side seam with very thin wire.

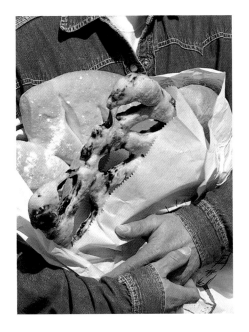

From May to September, starting with breakfast and rounding off the day with dinner under a setting sun, much of the time in Provence is spent outdoors. Living outside is elevated to an art form, whether in the garden or the village square, with areas for light and shade at different seasons and times of the day. Small tables are dotted around the garden to catch the early-morning sun or avoid it in the heat of the day. Shutters closed over south-facing windows in the morning are opened to let in the evening breeze. In villages, spreading plane trees offer dappled shade on a square, while a splashing fountain supplies the old *lavoir*, or wash house. The day starts with the market, which continues until noon when café tables are set out for lunch. At around four o'clock, younger children return from school, their play overlapping with an early-evening game of *pétanque* for the older villagers. The café and its terrace are the hub of Provençal life, a meeting place for young and old alike. **outdoors**

opposite A venerable plane tree offers shade for a tempting lunch table. **above** *Fougasse*, a Provençal bread eaten either with olives or *lardons*, herbs or cheese, is delicious fresh from the *boulangerie*.

right Shelter from the burning midday sun is a prerequisite in summer. Mats of woven straw or rushes slung casually on a trellis of metal poles provide patches of airy shade.

Fountains, springs and wells

Water is a valuable commodity in Provence, and many towns and villages are situated near natural springs. Aix, established by the Romans, is full of delightful and endearing fountains, while in the enchanting village of Cotignac, perched under a cliff, the spring waters rush directly through the village. Skilfully positioned to avoid the main flow, the houses all benefit from the availability and cooling effect of tumbling fresh water. To avoid misuse of this resource, the Provençal water code states that water must not be stored, the drainage system on every property must be maintained and nearby properties be notified of changes. Cotignac has a simple system of open water courses, in which each house has a small *bac d'eau*, a rectangular tank of water, which when full overflows into that of the next property down.

Fountains trickle and gurgle throughout the region, and were the only continuous water supply until 1956, when branches of the Canal de Verdon came fully into use. The lock-keeper would release the gates to regulate the hour-long flow of water allotted to each farmer to flood his fields. Now the Canal de Provence provides main irrigation outlets that distribute water on an account basis. But the fountains still stand as a picturesque reminder of earlier, harsher days. Carved from local stone, they are frequently double-sided – at the front are the decorative fountain and small basin, while in the rear is an overflow that runs into a larger lower basin, in which it was easy to prop a bucket or water a horse.

Where a well could be sunk, a farm would be built, and before 1956, the highest price for a farm was assessed according to the well's capacity. Water is an overriding concern, whether in order to contain its violence in the winter or to cope with its absence in the summer. Only 15 per cent of the rainfall comes in the months from May to September, and as the land becomes parched and tinder-dry, finding and storing water develops into an obsession. But in October when the heavens open, everyone makes feverish efforts to drain the excess water away from their land and property.

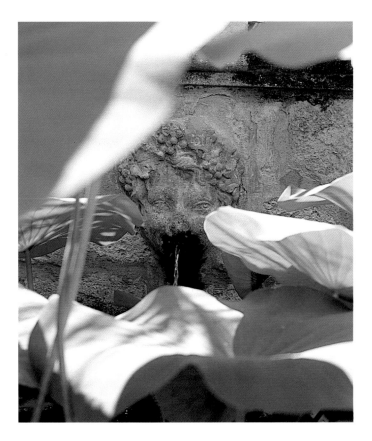

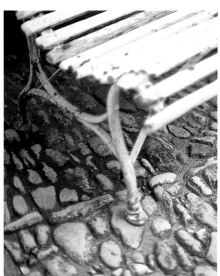

far left A carved stone head of Bacchus dribbles water among the luscious leaves of water lily and lotus.

left A *calade* or cobbled floor at Château de l'Ange, made with pebbles from the bed of the Durance river.

Lavender fields in full flower are one of the most beautiful sights in the world. In summer, the hills and valleys of Haute Provence are carpeted with row upon row of the fragrant purple bushes. First commercially cultivated in the early 1900s, Provençal lavender grown now accounts for 70 per cent of world production. Traditionally, lavender bushes were planted about 1m (39in) apart and harvested by hand. Today, however, the same space generally accommodates three bushes, and the flower spikes are cut by small tractors equipped with special blades. Lavender is harvested between June and September, when you can watch the slow procession of a tractor followed by a team of men who bundle up the cut lavender to dry in the warm sun. The air is filled with an intoxicating fragrance of freshly cut grass, dust and lavender, and some of this flavour is captured in the locally produced honey.

spot in the fields: lavender flowers in many different shades while *lavandin*, which can reproduce only by cloning, gives a uniform tone across the field. Lavender grows at much higher altitudes and is used for high-quality markets and particularly for essential oils; *lavandin* requires better soil and is used for commercial fragrances for soaps, powders and liquids.

To dry lavender, tie the flower spikes in loose bunches with an elastic band and hang them upside down in an airy, undisturbed place. When dry, rub the spikes until the flowers come away from the stalks. Use lavender in bags to scent cupboards and drawers. When the scent fades, rub and squeeze the bag: the warmth of your hand will release more fragrant essential oils.

To make a *fuseau* (see below), use only fresh lavender. You will need 1.8m (2yd) of ribbon that is 5mm (⅛in) wide. Place one end of the ribbon against the stalks, leaving 20cm (8in) hanging free for the final bow. Bend the stalks back over the lavender heads and secure them loosely in place. Then weave the rest of the ribbon in and out of the cage of lavender stalks to conceal the lavender flowers within. When all the ribbon is used, tie the two ends of the ribbon together in a bow.

far left Rolling across the landscape in stripes of glorious mauve, a field of lavender in bloom is a breath-taking sight.

left A lavender *fuseau* rests against a *boutis* cushion.

Distilling and drying lavender

Many of Provence's original lavender distilleries can still be found tucked among the hills, identifiable only by their tall chimneys. Two flowers are cultivated: natural lavender, representing 20 million francs' worth of business annually, and *lavandin*, a man-made mixture of natural lavender and spiked or English lavender, with sales figures of 150 million francs. The difference is easy to

above Harvesting flowers for perfume (here jasmine, with its intoxicating fragrance) is done by hand. The moment at which the blooms are ripe for picking is carefully judged.

above right Few scents are as evocative as that of a lime tree in full bloom under a sultry sun. The pale yellow flowers are used to make infusions or *tisanes*.

In Haute Provence, the gathering of medicinal and aromatic plants for perfumery and pharmacy is an age-old tradition. The *rose de mai* was introduced in the 1930s and is still grown around Grasse for the perfume industry. It takes 500kg (1,010lb) of rose petals to yield 1kg (2.2lb) of rose concentrate. To dry your own petals or herbs, gather only the best, discarding any that are discoloured. Dry them on an open basket tray to allow free circulation of air, then leave open as a potpourri or place in muslin bags for storage.

Wild herbs

Other wild plants that have been used to make herbal remedies over many generations are now commercially produced. Provençal mint is exceptionally fragrant and also yields menthol, used mainly in the food and pharmaceutical industries. Thyme is used in herbal teas and as a pungent seasoning in cooking; it is also a hearty stimulant and a powerful antiseptic. Lovers in Provence traditionally declared their suit by pinning a bouquet of thyme to the beloved's door. Clary sage, pretty but temperamental, is grown for its oils. Sage is grown for herbal teas, digestive wines and culinary uses. Rosemary is reputed to aid concentration and to relieve headaches, hair loss and dandruff.

left Rose petals
are spread out in airing
rooms and gently tossed
to disperse moisture.

below The famous
Savon de Marseille
contains a surprising
72 per cent olive oil.

Wines of Provence

Forty-five million cases of wine are produced annually in Provence, from a staggering 58 permitted grape varieties. From the red wines of the Châteauneuf-du-Pape vineyards near Avignon, the wine regions stretch down through the Coteaux d'Aix and the Côtes de Provence (producers of 60 per cent of Provence's rosé wine), on past Palette, dominated by the aromatic white wines of Château Simone, and down to the coastal regions of Cassis and Bandol, with their fruity fuller rosé wines.

Some of Provence's most outstanding wines come from the Domaine de Trévallon in the Coteaux des Baux, owned by Eloi and Floraine Durbach. Respected almost as a visionary by his peers, Eloi Durbach combines traditional and modern techniques, and his exceptional wines are now widely collected. A local favourite,

and more affordable, is the wine of Domaine les Bastides – the 'cuvée Valéria' produced by Jean Salen and his daughter Carole on the slopes north of Aix.

Provence now offers such a wealth of fine and interesting wines that it is helpful to seek advice. In Isle-sur-la-Sorgue in 1991, Robert Rocchi and his wife Noelle established an intimate wine bar, Le Caveau de la Tour de l'Isle, where they keep many bottles open for tasting. The wine is served by the glass with *tapenade* (a purée of black olives) and goat's cheese nibbles, as customers compare and recommend wines. The *bar à vin* is stacked high with bottles, while on the other side three large vats containing local wines are decanted straight into 5-litre *bidons*. Since Robert's prices are those of the vineyards, his clientele is faithful: at Sunday market time it is almost impossible to squeeze in for a glass or two.

opposite Freshly picked grapes await crushing.

left Vats hold wine that has come directly from the vineyards, leaving the customer to do the bottling.

above Robert Rocchi fills a client's 5-litre *bidon* with a local red, selected as both good and inexpensive.

Olives

The olive tree is the signature of Provence, the symbol of peace and eternity (it can live for a thousand years, after all). Olive trees grow slowly and their root system remains relatively compact, so ancient trees can be transported and re-established elsewhere. Contrary to popular belief, olive trees can and do survive temperatures below freezing. But on 9 February 1956, in the Pays d'Aix, a day when many people still recall 'working outside with shirtsleeves rolled up at two o'clock in the afternoon' at 16°C, the temperature plummeted within hours to −4°C, and most of the olive and almond trees apparently perished. The almond trees were removed, but the olive trees were simply cut back – and the following spring new shoots pushed out, though the main tree trunks were dead. France now produces only 2 per cent of its olive oil consumption, some 2,475 tonnes, used mostly for extra virgin, fine virgin or semi-virgin olive oil.

Olives are still gathered in traditional fashion by pickers perched on tapering ladders, who pull rakes through the branches to shake the olives into baskets around their necks or onto large sheets spread under the trees. At the mill, the olives are crushed

by stone wheels to a fine paste. This is then spread over round woven hemp mats, or *scourtins*, and pressed to release a mixture of oil and water, which are separated in a centrifuge to produce 'cold-pressed' olive oil. The olives can be used a second time, but the most expensive oil comes from the first pressing.

Of the hundred or so existing varieties of olives, eight are normally used in Provence. Each variety produces small white flowers in the spring, followed by green olives which turn black as

opposite The medal of the Confrérie des Chevaliers de l'Olivier is worn with pride.

centre Olive picking is still done entirely by hand in Provence, in order to conserve both the olives and the trees. The pickers rake the branches, pulling the olives into baskets slung about their necks or onto sheets spread beneath the trees.

tapenade

Tapenade is a favourite olive recipe, though the name is derived from *tapéno*, Provençal for caper. Most prepared *tapenade* in tins is ground to a fine paste; I prefer the rougher texture obtained when all the ingredients are pummelled with a pestle in a stone mortar. With its pungent taste and aroma, *tapenade* is a perfect match for pastis, served on toasted rounds of baguette. It is also used as an ingredient in numerous recipes and is quite delicious. Kept in an airtight container in the refrigerator, freshly made *tapenade* will last for two to three weeks.

ingredients and method

Blend together 500g (20oz) stoned black or green olives, 100g (4oz) anchovy fillets in oil, 100g (4oz) capers and 2 cloves of garlic to form a paste. Stir in a dribble of olive oil to make the mixture looser, and add lemon juice and black pepper to taste.

they mature. *La salonenque* is a variety picked in the autumn months while they are green, then half crushed and mixed with fennel stalks and seeds: each of these olives contains 75 per cent water and 15 per cent oil. *L'aglandeau*, a black olive used for oil, is by contrast 3 per cent water and 55 per cent oil, and is gathered during the winter months. Rich in vitamin E with provitamin A, with a high non-saturated fat content, olive oil is a gourmet delight that also makes for healthy eating.

right A market stall in autumn, boasting a large and decorative pumpkin – used to make delicious soup – and varieties of garlic. Markets in Provence are a year-round affair.

opposite Delicious Cavaillon melons, with distinctive orange flesh; little round courgettes, a Provençal speciality that are perfect for barbecues as they do not fall through the grill; and *petits poivrons*, or little sweet peppers, grown on dwarf plants and pretty enough to grace a window box.

Markets

Every village in Provence has its market day, when local produce is piled in tempting heaps on wonderfully colourful stalls. Larger towns may have several market days specializing in different wares. Market produce is neither less nor more expensive than that in hypermarkets and there are bargains to be had at both. On market day the town centre comes to life early: cars are removed, the vans roll in, the trestle tables unfold, the parasols and awnings go up and the wares are displayed. Local people know the stallholders' names and are known by name in return – there is nothing impersonal about going to market.

Everything can be bought at the market, from flowers to sunhats and from chickens, ducks and rabbits to seasonal specialities. Fruit and vegetables are picked that morning or the day before, with no need for plastic trays or cling-film wrapping. The smells are enveloping, whether of live goats waiting to be sold, of chicken roasting on spits, or of herbs laid out in fabric-lined baskets. Selecting your own produce in metal bowls means you can examine every item by sight, smell and touch. The fishmonger will prepare and season the fish, offering tempting recipes on request. Everything is well labelled with its local origin, and prices are clearly marked. It is always worth wandering through the whole market and comparing prices before you buy, and remember that prices frequently fall at noon when the stallholders start packing up. Then everyone retires to the café for an *apéro* or lunch and a chance to compare the morning's spoils. Heaters are brought out in the winter and parasols in the summer, and people stay outside. Markets are a source of unfailing fascination, culinary delights and many a treasured bargain for summer visitors. But for the locals they are an essential part of life throughout the year. Perhaps the most important market day throughout Provence is on 4 December, the feast of Sainte Barbe, when special markets in the larger towns sell everything from luxury foods, *foie gras*, truffles and chocolates to clothes of every size and description. Traditional Provençal *santons* often have their own special place at these markets, where they will remain until the New Year.

right Powdered spices amd flasks of flavoured oil in a tempting display on a market stall.

centre Fresh goat's and sheep's cheeses are delicious both plain and flavoured with herbs and spices.

Fresh from the boulangerie

Two delicious and very Provençal specialities on sale at many *boulangeries* are *fougasse* and *navettes*; both are served as apéritifs. *Fougasse* is large, oval and flat with slashes gaping to reveal the filling inside. Each *boulangerie* has its favourite fillings, but the most usual are olives and anchovies, bacon and cheese, and any other little leftovers that can be wrapped in scraps of dough and baked, which is how *fougasse* came into being.

Navettes are small, lozenge-shaped biscuits normally served with pastis. Dry and delicately flavoured, they contain orange flower water and a little orange zest, which harmonizes well with the aniseed aroma and taste of pastis. Named after the little ferry boat (*navette*) that, according to religious belief, brought Saint Mary to Provence, the biscuits are also traditionally served on 2 February when the *santons* of the Nativity are turned with their backs to the *crèche* in a gesture symbolizing the banishment of homelessness.

goat's cheese in olive oil with herbs

For centuries the people of Provence have used this simple
way of preserving the summer's goat's cheeses for consumption
during the leaner winter months. The marinated cheese
is delicious served with a green salad.

ingredients and method

Fill a wide-necked glass jar with small goat's cheeses.
Add 4–5 sprigs each of thyme, bay, rosemary and summer
savory, 10–12 whole black peppercorns, and fill with olive oil.
Cover and keep for at least a month before serving.

Goat's cheeses

Throughout Provence, goat's and sheep's cheeses are sold in a
bewildering variety of shapes and coverings. Goat's cheese is highly
local in Provence, and individual market stalls will sell their own
farm cheeses. The white little cheeses may be sprinkled with wood
cinders, paprika, crushed black and red peppercorns, raisins and
sultanas soaked in *marc*, or fresh herbs – notably *sarriette*, or
summer savory, renowned for making donkeys frisky. Market
stallholders sell their goat's cheeses in three stages: fresh (one to
three days old), with a creamy coat; several days to a week old;
and *sec* (dried out), with a stronger flavour and crumbly texture.

André Gouiran tends one of the last herds of 200 goats that
over the centuries have adapted to this arid land, with its lack of
water and little vegetation. The goats, with wonderful long lyre-
shaped horns and coats of fawn and black, scamper sure-footedly
over the cliffs during the day. The milk is transformed into
uncooked cheese, which is drained into a perforated cone rather
than being pressed. It is very light and delicious when sprinkled
with fresh herbs or orange flower water. Banon is a goat's cheese
wrapped in chestnut leaves, tied with raffia and placed in an
earthenware pot for storage into the winter months. Fresh baby
rounds of goat's cheese can also be stored in olive oil with a variety
of seasonings, including fresh whole black and red peppercorns,
thyme, rosemary, bay, juniper berries or garlic (see above).

right *Rascasse* and a cornucopia of other fish glisten in the fish market on the quay of the old port in Marseille.

centre At the early morning market, fish is unloaded direct from the boats onto the waiting market stalls.

opposite Fishing boats are moored while the fishermen catch up on sleep before the next night's work.

Bouillabaisse 'Chez Fonfon', for 6 people

For the fish soup, prepare a stock from 2kg (4½lb)of bony little *rascasse* (in English, scorpion or rockfish) with the head and tail of a *congre* or conger eel, gutted and rinsed. In olive oil in a large casserole brown 3 chopped onions, 6 cloves of garlic, 4 large tomatoes peeled and chopped, and 2 full bulbs of fennel, chopped. Stir in 2 bay leaves, 500g (18oz) tomato purée, 4 sprigs of thyme, and parsley, salt, pepper and saffron. Add the *rascasse* and *congre*, cover with water and bring to the boil, then continue to simmer and reduce the stock for at least 40 minutes, stirring to release all the flavours of the small fish. Let it cool and strain the stock, pressing the pulp of vegetables through.

Return the stock to the casserole dish and bring to the boil with 200g (8oz) of potatoes, peeled and cut thick. Then add the main five fish. At Chez Fonfon, these are the body of the conger, 1.5kg (3¼ lb) John Dory (*saint pierre*), 500g (18oz) monkfish (*lotte* or locally *la baudroie*), 500g (18oz) gurnard (locally *galinette* or *rouget grondin*), 500g (18oz) of weever fish (locally *araignée* or *vive*) all gutted and scaled.

Place the larger and less delicate fish to cook in the stock, then add the tender smaller fish according to their individual requirements, to a maximum of 15 minutes.

Bouillabaisse is always served in a generous bowl: the fish soup stock first, with *croûtons* rubbed with a clove of garlic, and *'la rouille'* a mayonnaise base with crushed garlic, saffron strands and cayenne pepper added. The fish is served on an open plate, to be boned and selected at table.

Bouillabaisse is the famous Provençal fish stew long associated with Marseille, although it has always been enjoyed further afield. Originally it was cooked close to the fishermen's cabins on the beach, in a large cauldron suspended over a wood fire. The fish stock was made from any fish that was unsold or too small to be sold. Any more choice fish that remained was then introduced on a daily basis, cooked in the prepared cauldron stock. The name is a contraction of *bouillir*, to boil, and *abaisser*, to reduce: in Provençal *boui-abaisso*, hence bouillabaisse. Many variations of the recipe exist, as is natural given the essentially ad hoc nature of the original dish. In 1980, however, some of the restaurateurs of Marseilles signed a 'bouillabaisse charter', designed to protect and defend the 'authentic' recipe. Among the signatories to the charter are Roger and Alexandre Pinna of the restaurant Chez Fonfon. Chez Fonfon stands in an idyllic position on a charming fishing cove, with small fishermen's cabins (*lou cabanoun*) and fishing boats jostling for space in the tiny harbour known as Le Vallon des Auffes. Given the opportunity to buy the local bar, Alexandre's great-uncle developed the restaurant that exists today. Alexandre never questioned his calling, and he and his family now run an exceptional fish restaurant, taking full advantage of the day's catch as it is brought in, fresh from the sea. At Chez Fonfon the recipe for bouillabaisse remains constant. Alexandre respects his clients' desire to taste a 'true' Fonfon bouillabaisse, but openly admits that for family and friends he enjoys being more flexible, adding whatever is available in the fish-market.

above The central cross lath of willow is opened out like spokes of a wheel. Additional stake willows are inserted to create the basket sides.

above right Siding up the stakes creates the depth of the basket.

basket maker

In Vallabrègues, one of the close-knit villages past which the mighty Rhône surges between Arles and Avignon, Ernest Dettinger works with his wife Jany, herself the daughter of a basket weaver. Before the construction of the hydroelectric dam here, the village stood on an island planted with cherry trees and willow. Willow is a particularly light, supple, hard wearing and versatile material, perfect for weaving baskets for a variety of purposes. It can be worked either stripped of bark, giving a bleached smooth appearance, or green, straight from the tree.

After the flooding of the river banks, the cherry pickers needed fewer baskets, the fishermen's need for mussel and fish baskets dwindled, and the basket makers' once-abundant raw materials lay submerged. Traditional basket-weaving skills almost disappeared, but some years ago the village's inspired mayor decided to celebrate its long history with an annual festival each second weekend in August. Old and new baskets are now once more heaped onto horse-drawn carts and paraded through the streets, accompanied by people dressed in clothes that belonged to their grandparents' – and, of course, carrying a basket.

centre Ernest works comfortably seated since an olive basket takes several hours to complete.

below Basketwork protects glass wine casks and provides convenient carrying handles.

arch fountain surround

materials and tools
several 3-cm (1¼-in)
thick sheets of white
polystyrene, normal
cement
(for backdrop),
paint, paintbrush,
water-resistant
ready-made cement
(for basin),
craft knife,
tacks, trowel,
rag, sandpaper
or wire brush
(to rub down paint).

Now that water is piped from the mains to almost every house, the significance of the old fountains in every town and village is often forgotten. With a little determination and muscle power, however, it is possible to install your own fountain and enjoy the soothing gurgle of trickling water. Unless you happen to have a spring, you will need a pump to circulate the water for your fountain. Look for the new solar pumps that circulate the water on sunny days, when you are most likely to be in the garden, and avoid the additional expense of providing electricity at a distance from the house. There are many possibilities for water-collecting basins, from hewn stone to grey breeze blocks covered in cement. All will work, as long as they are large and deep enough to conceal the pump. When installing any open water system outdoors, consider covering the water with a metal grille for the safety of small children. Your builder or garden centre should stock everything you need for making fountains. When you have selected your basin, plumb it in and conceal the pipes with mortar. Consider buying some water lilies and other water plants, which look most attractive and help hide the pump. Seal the interior of the basin with water-resistant ready-made cement, smoothing it level for ease of future cleaning. An occasional cup of bleach in the water will deter algae and wasps.

step one Cut 3-cm (1¼-in) thick polystyrene to act as an outer frame and tack it to the wall. In the design area, tack in nails to protrude just under 3cm (1in) – these mean the cement can be applied uniformly over a large area while the polystyrene contains the cement edge.

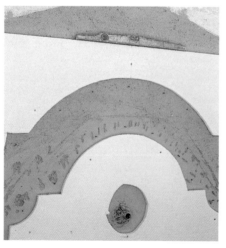

step two Leave to dry out thoroughly. To create the ochre arch in relief that is typical of Provence, repeat the design procedure, cutting another polystyrene template. Once again, tack in nails to ensure that there is an even application of cement.

step three Let the cement dry out thoroughly before painting. Traditional paints have local sand and soil mixed in to create stunning colours. When you have finished, remove the templates, replace the fountainhead and let the water trickle and fill the basin.

herb garden pebbled footpath

Throughout Provence, pebbles are pressed into cement to make decorative surfaces. They are both inexpensive and attractive, and I only wish I had saved all those offered to me by my small children over the years. They may come from the beach or from the broad bed of the Durance river that traverses much of Provence. These pebble tiles are easy to make, and at 40 x 40 x 3cm (16 x 16 x 1¼in) are large enough to give room to walk on and to allow herbs to flourish.

Provence is justly famous for its herbs, both savoury and sweet, and used not only in the garden but also in the house. At Christmas, *santon* figures are placed on moss with minute hedgerows of lavender and trees of tied thyme; cupboards have little scented lavender bags tucked into the corners; and dried herbs hang from the kitchen rafters.

On planting herbs in my little vegetable garden, I was amazed at how large they grew: while herbs will tolerate a bad soil, they flourish in a good one. Surprisingly, they do not enjoy too much sun: growing wild over the *garrigue* of hilly inland provinces, they enjoy the shade of native trees such as oak, olive and pine. When you have selected an area to suit them, clear the ground and level it. The tiles are heavy and should settle well, but if necessary can be lifted and a little earth added beneath.

materials and tools
3 x 3cm (1¼ x 1¼in) pine wood, plastic bags or sheeting, string, chicken wire, white cement and sand, pebbles, mixing bucket and old towel, kitchen scissors or pliers.

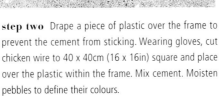

step one To make frames, cut lengths of wood to an inside measurement of 40cm (16in). For each tile, place four lengths of wood in a square on level ground and secure the outside with string to form a frame. Make two frames for 10kg (22lb) cement.

step two Drape a piece of plastic over the frame to prevent the cement from sticking. Wearing gloves, cut chicken wire to 40 x 40cm (16 x 16in) square and place over the plastic within the frame. Mix cement. Moisten pebbles to define their colours.

step three Pour cement up to the frame level. As it dries, pop the pebbles in to half their depth – if one sinks too far, retrieve and rinse it, wait a while and continue. Leave overnight. Undo the string, ease the frame and plastic away. Prop against a wall to dry thoroughly.

craft address book

Pigment

Blancolor offers a varied choice of colours in many finishes, both for interiors and exteriors. Advice is supplied in good step-by-step leaflets.

S.A. Blancolor, Rue de Mousselière, 30133 Les Angles, France.

tel: 00 33 4 90 15 22 50

email: info@blancolor.com.

The Conservatoire des Ochres et Pigments appliqués in the Usine Mathieu is open for sales and visits all year round (visits by appointment in December and January) and offers workshops and courses in the use of ochres and pigments.

Conservatoire des Ochres et Pigments appliqués, Usine Mathieu, D104, 94220 Roussillon, France.

tel and fax: 00 33 4 90 05 66 69

Abigail Saint George paints wonderful and intriguing *trompe l'oeil* (see pages 20, 28-29). She is available for courses and commissions.

1620 Chemin Barthélémy Véra, 13290 Aix-les-Milles, France.

email: asaintgeor@aol.com

Daler-Rowney fine art materials are distributed worldwide. Working with these high-quality products gives the best results. A full 128-page catalogue shows the range of products available and offers constructive advice as to their uses.

Daler-Rowney House, Bracknell, Berkshire RG12 8ST, England.

tel: 01344 424621

web site: www.daler-rowney.com

Ceramics

Alain and Jacotte Vagh offer a large selection of terracotta and glazed tiles, in a variety of shapes and sizes. They include most of the tiles shown in this book. The family-run business also provides advice on selection and design. Tiles are hand-painted, and clients can participate in the design process. These tiles are sold in outlets throughout the world.

Alain Vagh, Route d'Entrecasteaux, 83690, Salernes, France.

tel: 00 33 4 94 70 61 85

web site alainvagh.com

Denis Aune at **Les Poseurs de Salernes** offers expert advise and beautiful tile laying.

Quartier Le Serre, 83690 Salernes, France.

tel and fax: 00 33 4 94 70 72 97

Santon Fouque, open throughout the year, is a charming little workshop producing many hundreds of models, with continuous demonstrations and explanations of the techniques involved.

Santon Fouque, 65 Cours Gambetta, Route de Nice, 13100 Aix-en-Provence, France.

tel: 00 33 4 42 26 33 38

Poteries Ravel is an inspiration to gardeners, offering beautiful terracotta pots in every shape and size. These traditional Provençal jars and pots are fascinating in their range and diversity.

Poteries Ravel, Avenue des Goums, 13400 Aubagne, France.

tel: 00 33 4 42 82 42 00

Fabrics

Souleiado features collections of Provençal fabrics in traditional and contemporary designs and various weights of material. They include many of the fabrics shown in this book. The Souleiado shops, throughout France and in the world's major capital cities, are a feast of colourful fabrics not to be missed.

Souleiado Museum and Head Office, 39 Rue Proudhon, 13150 Tarascon, France.

tel (reception): 00 33 4 90 91 50 11

Edith Mezard's embroidery studio, set in a converted stable building, offers both ready-to-embroider and finished pieces. Embroidery commissions for wedding trousseaus, baby clothes, table and bed linen (see pages 67-69).

Château de l'Ange 84220, Lumières, France.

tel: 00 33 4 90 72 36 41

DMC offers a choice of over 428 colours in pearl, stranded and sewing thread, as well as a good choice of fabric weaves and textures for embroidery. A comprehensive catalogue and colour charts are available.

DMC, 62 Pullman Road, Widston, Leicester LE18 2DY, England.

tel: 0116 2811040

Manual Canovas stocks the *toile de Jouy* fabric used for the quilted bedcover (see pages 72-73).

Manuel Canovas, 2 North Terrace, Brompton Road, London SW3 2BA, England.

tel: 020 7225 2298

And

7 rue Furstenberg, 75006 Paris, France.

tel: 0033 1 43 25 75 98

Furniture

Bruno Carles provides expert advice on all Provençal antiques. His shop offers a great variety of Provençal furniture, from large cupboards to small items. Bruno also makes his own furniture, adapting traditional Provençal designs for contemporary use.

Bruno Carles Antiques,
209-235 Avenue
du Marechal de Lattre de Tassigny,
34400 Lunel, France.
tel: 00 33 4 67 71 36 10
web site: www.brunocarles.fr.

The **Monleau** family has been making Provençal and Camarguaises chairs for five generations in the small town of Vallabrègues (see pages 88-89).

Monleau, 44 Rue Nationale,
30300 Vallabrègues, France.
tel and fax: 00 33 4 66 59 20 17

Vincent Mit l'Ane sells antiques and makes Provençal chairs. The project on painted furniture (see pages 90-91) uses Vincent's light, curvaceous designs.

Vincent Mit l'Ane,
5 Avenue des 4 Otages,
L'Isle-sur-la-Sorgue, France.
tel: 00 33 4 90 20 63 15

Metalwork

La Ferronnerie de Provence offered generous help and much-appreciated expertise during the preparation of this book.

La Ferronnerie de Provence,
95 Rue Victor Baltard,
13852 Aix-les-Milles, France.
tel: 00 33 4 42 39 44 98

Fermob supplies metal tables and chairs in traditional and contemporary styles, producing beautiful furniture that is also robust enough to resist the mistral wind. A catalogue is available.

Fermob, 21 St Didier, BP 8,
01140 Thoissey, France.
tel: 00 33 4 74 69 71 98

Swish stocks an exceptional selection of iron curtain rails, of good quality and workmanship. Swish products are available from:

Newell Window Fashions,
Lichfield Road Industrial Estate,
Tamworth, Staffs.,
B79 7TW, England.
tel: 01827 64242

Outdoors

Visit **Robert Rocchi** for an excellent and varied selection of wines, at the Caveau de La Tour de L'Isle.

Le Caveau de La Tour de L'Isle,
12 Rue de la Republique,
84800 L'Isle-sur-la-Sorgue, France.
tel: 00 33 4 90 20 70 25

Chez Fonfon offers delicious food in picturesque surroundings. The fish is brought straight from the harbour into the kitchen, and the bouillabaisse is a must.

Chez Fonfon, 140 Rue du Vallon des Auffes,
13007 Marseille, France.
tel 00 33 4 91 52 14 38

At **La Boutique de la Vannerie**, Ernest Dettinger sits weaving baskets for olives, cherries or daily shopping. Baskets can be made to order in most weaving materials.

La Boutique de la Vannerie, 6 Rue Carnot,
30300 Vallabrègues, France.
tel: 00 33 4 66 59 62 08

Pierre Carron has a talent for working with stone. For the fountain project (see page 136-137), he worked with cement to create a wonderfully curvaceous fountain back.

Pierre Carron, 12 Lotissement la Tubier,
13650 Meyrargues, France.
tel: 00 33 4 42 63 42 58

For details of courses on Provençal crafts, cooking and gardening, visit Amelia Saint George's website: www.ameliasaintgeorge.com.

index

Page numbers in *italic* refer to the illustrations

Acknowledgments

Author's Acknowledgments

I should like to thank the following individuals and organizations for their help and invaluable advise: Association 'Li Venturie', Oustau de Prouvenco, Parc Jourdan, 6 bis Avenue Jules Ferry, 13100 Aix-en-Provence. Here you can learn about every aspect of Provence, from the language and cuisine to *boutis* work.

Bibliothèque des Métiers d'Art in Aix-en-Provence, and in particular Béatrice Coignet, who could not have been more helpful or accommodating with research and additional ideas.

Pierre Bonnet, for his tireless search for authentic Provençal items. A delightfully kind and bubbly man, Pierre runs the Hotel de Guilles at Lourmarin, which makes the perfect base for discovering Provence, tel: 00 33 4 90 68 30 55 and 00 33 4 90 68 21 04, fax: 00 33 4 90 68 37 41.

Pierre Armitano, for carefully checking over various details and being a wonderful neighbour. Pierre Barnier, for historic local gossip that proved both helpful and amusing. Katherine and Daniel, for use of location and the hens. And last but not least, Elisabeth Pathieu, for being an Arlésienne who discovered more about placing her shawl.

Picture Acknowledgments in page order

1-3 Pierre Hussenot/Agence Top; 4 Deidi von Schaewen; 6 Mick Rock/Cephas; 7 H. Daries/Agence Top; 8 above, Yves Duronsoy; 8 centre, Gerard Sieon/Agence Top; 9 above, Yves Duronsoy; 10 Pascal Chevalier/Agence Top; 12 Richard Turpin/Aspect; 12-13 N. Jaubert/Image du Sud; 13 Eric Morin; 14 Michael Busselle; 15 David Martin Hughes/Robert Harding Picture Library; 16 Nick Wheeler/Robert Harding Picture Library; 17 Robert Harding Picture Library; 18 Christian Sarramon; 19 Pierre Putelat/ Agence Top; 21 above, Richard Turpin/Aspect; 21 below, Christian Sarramon; 22 left, Guillaum de Laubier/INSIDE; 22 right, Pascal Chevalier/Agence Top; 24 P. Saharoff/INSIDE; 24-25 J.P. Godeaut/INSIDE; 25 Pascal Chevallier/Agence Top; 32 Maison Francaise/F. Lemarchand/INSIDE; 34 left Norma Joseph/Robert Harding Picture Library; 35 Herve Champollion/Cephas; 38 Maison Francaise/ F. Lemarchand/INSIDE; 41 Yves Duronsoy; 43 Pierre Hussenot/Agence Top/Cephas; 44 left, Christian Sarramon; 44 right, and 45 Eric Morin; 46 left and 47 right, Gerard Sioen/Agence Top; 56 above, Pascal Hinous/Agence Top; 59 Yves Duronsoy; 60 above, Gerard Sioen/Agence Top; 60 below, Richard Turpin/Aspect; 60-61 Eric Morin; 62 left and right, Christian Sarramon; 63 Pascal Hinous/Agence Top; 64-65 Yves Douronsoy; 74 J.P Godeaut/INSIDE; 75 Robert Harding; 76-77 Deidi von Schaewen; 77 Christian Sarramon; 78 Gerard Sioen/Agence Top; 79 left, Pascal Chevalier/Agence Top; 82 left, Roland Beaufre/Agence Top; 84 left, Eric Morin; 84 right, Yves Duronsoy; 85 Yves Duronsoy; 96 right, and 97 Deidi von Schaewen; 99 Pierre Putelat/Agence Top; 100 left, J.P. Godeaut/INSIDE (Maison Michel Sambona); 100 right - 102 Gerard Sioen/Agence Top; 103 left, Richard Turpin/Aspect; 103 right, Pierre Putelat/Agence Top; 104 Eric Morin; 105 left, Christian Sarramon; 105 right, Deidi von Schaewen; 106 John Sims/Anthony Blake Photo Library; 107 Christophe Bluntzer/IMPACT; 109 right, Pascal Chevalier (Nicole de Vesian)/Agence Top; 116 Christian Sarramon; 117 Eric Morin; 118 F. Lemarchand/Maison Francaise/INSIDE; 121 Yves Duronsoy; 122 left, H. Daries/Agence Top; 122 right, Gerard Sioen/Agence Top; 123 H. Daries/ Agence Top; 124 Michael Busselle/Robert Harding; 126 Pierre Hussenot/Agence Top/Cephas; 126-127 Pierre Hussenot/Agence Top; 128 Nigel Blythe/Cephas; 132-133 H. Daries/Agence Top; 133 Tipeleon/Jarry/Agence Top/Cephas.

The photographs on the following pages were taken specially for Conran Octopus by:

Yves Duronsoy; 2, 8 below, 11, 20, 33, 34 right, 36, 37, 39, 40, 42, 44 centre, 46 right, 47 left, 48-49, 54-55, 80-81, 86-87, 94-96 left, 98, 102 right, 108, 119 left, 129, 130 left, 132.

Michelle Garrett; 5, 9 below, 23, 26-31, 50-53, 56 below-58, 61, 66 right-73, 82 right -83, 88-93, 100 centre 109 - 113, 119 right, 121, 123 right, 125, 127, 130-131, 134-139.

Helen Fickling; 114-115.